KINDLY
SIT DOWN!

KINDLY SIT DOWN!

*Best After-Dinner Stories
from both Houses of Parliament*

Compiled by
JACK ASPINWALL, MP
Illustrated by Timothy Jaques

BUCHAN & ENRIGHT, PUBLISHERS
LONDON

First published in 1983 by
Buchan & Enright, Publishers, Limited
53 Fleet Street, London EC4Y 1BE

ISBN 0 907675 09 3

*In the course of the production of this book there have been a number
of changes of Members' positions in the Houses of Parliament. While
every effort has been made to keep up with these changes, it has,
inevitably, not been possible to make all the necessary alterations.*

Photoset in North Wales by
Derek Doyle & Associates, Mold, Clwyd
Printed in Great Britain by
Richard Clay (The Chaucer Press) Ltd
Bungay, Suffolk

FOREWORD
by
the Right Honourable
Margaret Thatcher, MP

As one who finds herself on her feet during speeches after dinner, rather than sitting down and having to listen to the speeches, I believe that I have a vested interest in seeing that the customers who have to be at the receiving end of such speeches get the best possible service.

It was, after all, the late Governor Adlai Stevenson who defined a politician as one who approached every question with an open mouth. He went on to talk of a Presidential Candidate, who was then barnstorming across the continent of the United States as being engaged in a 'ghost to ghost tour' and having in the course of his speeches succeeded in 'passing the 49th platitude'.

So politicians – and all public speakers – are clearly greatly in need of being able to salt their after-dinner speeches with a bit of savoury humour, and I am sure that this book – whether as pure entertainment or as a source – is going to be very much in demand by politicians and non-politicians alike. I am glad the main proceeds of this book will be going to the Airey Neave Memorial Trust which is such a worthy and excellent cause, and I wish the book every success.

Margaret Thatcher

INTRODUCTION
Jack Aspinwall, MP

Whilst lying in the Cambridge Military Hospital, Aldershot, recovering from a compressed fracture of the spine after a sponsored parachute jump in aid of charity that, for me had gone disastrously wrong, I became determined to be successful in at least something. I thought about editing a book of after-dinner stories – the material to come from my excellent colleagues in Parliament (and others), all to raise funds for the Airey Neave Memorial Trust and other charities.

This is what I have done, and I am very grateful indeed to all those many people who have made contributions, not least because the favourite after-dinner story is probably the most prized possession of a Parliamentarian.

This book, *Kindly Sit Down!*, has many purposes, perhaps spreading a little humour, raising funds for charities, and possibly helping those who may be involved in speech-making for the first time. The main proceeds will go to the Airey Neave Memorial Trust and the Airey Neave Refugee Trust, to further their causes and as a memorial to the late Airey Neave, DSO, OBE, MC, TD, MP, Member of Parliament for Abingdon from 1953 until his tragic assassination at the Palace of Westminster on 30 March 1979. I have had the privilege of studying his life and work, and I am proud to be associated with an organisation which commemorates his life.

The other charities expected to benefit will be those connected with children, cancer research and the care of the elderly.

There is nothing like the glimpse of the fire to reconcile people to the frying pan.

After a long spell in hospital that followed my parachuting accident, when I sustained a fractured spine, I became an out-patient at a local hospital. One day I was sitting on a bench alongside an old lady wearing a surgical collar around her neck. We eventually got talking, and I asked her what was wrong with her. She replied she had fallen down the stairs and chipped a bone in her back. Inevitably came the question 'What happened to you?' I thought for a moment and told her that I had fallen out of an aeroplane. The old lady looked carefully around and then said, 'I think you have come to the wrong place. This is the Physiotherapy Department—the Psychiatric Wing is on the other side of the hospital!'

My wife, Brenda, was introduced to a colleague of mine in the Central Lobby of the House of Commons. After much hand-shaking and kisses on both cheeks, my colleague asked my wife how her feet were now? Somewhat indignantly, she replied that her feet were fine, and what did my friend mean? He replied very gracefully that he thought they might have been bruised when she fell down from heaven!

An ornithologist crossed a carrier pigeon with a woodpecker, producing a bird that would not only carry messages, but would also knock on doors when it arrived!

Lord Denning, PC, DL Master of the Rolls until 1982
This is a letter which I received from the International Students' House. I introduce it by saying that some people, even in London, do not know who the Master of the Rolls is:

Dear Lord Denning,
  I am an Indian citizen. I graduated in Mechanical

2

Engineering in the University of London and was awarded a Master of Science degree. I feel I have the necessary qualifications, motivation, energy, drive and personality to begin a successful career in an automobile industry. I will ever remain grateful to you if you would kindly help me to begin my professional career with your Company, the Rolls-Royce Motor Company ...

So he thought that I was either the Chairman of the Company or the driver of one of their cars.

Ron Dearing, CB Chairman, Post Office

The Post Office undoubtedly performs many social roles but seldom does it ever go as far as it did in a large sorting office a few days ago where a letter arrived addressed to 'God in Heaven'. Having sorted all the other letters, the postmen in the office gathered around in a group and one of them opened the letter.

Inside was a conventional note with the writer's home address in the top right hand corner (including the postcode of course). The postman read it out to his colleagues. It read:

Dear God. I am in desperate trouble and I need £30 to get out of it. If you can let me have £30 I promise to become a better Christian, to pray every night and to go to Church every Sunday.

The staff, in their usual warm-hearted way, had a collection and raised £12. They turned the money into notes, put them into an envelope, addressed it to the man and posted it again with a first class stamp.

The following night, at the same sorting office, the same staff saw another letter addressed to 'God in Heaven'. Once

3

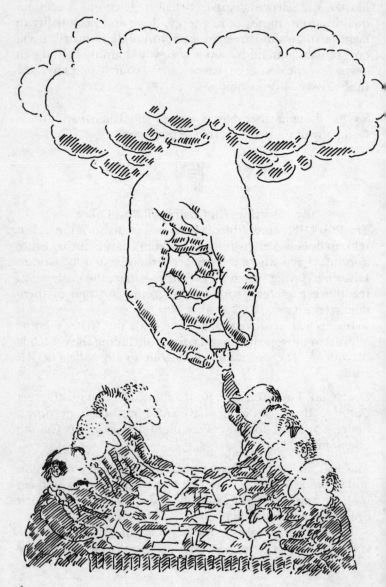

again, having done their job, they gathered round. The letter was opened and read to the group. It read:

Dear God. Thank you very much for the £12 you sent me. I did ask for £30. I did need £30. I have no doubt that you sent £30, and that those thieving so-and-sos in the Post Office took the rest.

Eric P. Cockeram, JP, MP

Picture two gates to Heaven, one with the notice: 'Queue here all men who are henpecked by their wives', the other carrying the notice: 'Queue here all men who are not henpecked by their wives'. St Peter arrived at the gates one morning to find a long queue of men trailing into the distance behind the former gate and one small insignificant looking man standing behind the second gate. On enquiring from him as to his qualifications for seeking entry through that gate, he replied, 'I really don't know, my wife told me to come and queue here.'

Lord Barber, PC, TD

At every meeting which the by-election candidate had held, his speech was ruined by a little old lady who followed him around. She always sat in the front row and, just as he was making his final remarks, would invariably shout out, 'If you were the Archangel Gabriel, I wouldn't vote for you!'

'If I were the Archangel Gabriel,' he replied, 'it is most unlikely that you would be living in my constituency!'

Lord Aberdare, PC

An English tourist, who rather fancied his meagre knowledge of French, went over on a day trip to Calais and had a meal in a restaurant. He found a fly in his soup and summoned the waiter by calling out a very Anglicised version of 'Garçon'. When the waiter arrived, he pointed at the fly floating in the soup and said repeatedly, 'Le mouch, le mouch!' The waiter with great dignity replied, 'Excusez-moi, Monsieur. C'est la mouche.' 'Good heavens,' said the diner, 'I must say, you Frenchmen have marvellous eyesight!'

Sir Philip de Zulueta, Kt

There is an American story about a petitioner before a US Internal Revenue Court who observed, 'As God is my Judge, I do not owe the tax assessed.' The Judge replied with commendable brevity, 'He is not, I am, you do.'

Lord Grey of Naunton, GCMG, GCVO, OBE

An Englishman, a Scotsman and an Irishman were cast away on a desert island. In that unpromising environment the myths of history were forgotten and they lived amicably, although restlessly, together. One day, rooting rather aimlessly in the sand, they came upon a metallic object which proved to be an ancient brass lamp. By rubbing the sand off, it produced the inevitable Genie. He said, 'I can give you fellows three wishes, that is, one each, fulfilment of which is guaranteed.'

The Englishman immediately wished that he be returned to his loving wife and family, and he left. The Scotsman said that he could not improve on the Englishman's wish, and he too vanished. After an anxious pause for consideration, the Irishman said, 'I shall be so lonely here without my two friends that I wish them back again.'

William Wormald

A man went into Harrods' vegetable department and was heard to have the following conversation:

CUSTOMER: 'Two avocados, please.'

SALESMAN: 'Yes, Sir, large or small?'

CUSTOMER: 'Large.'

SALESMAN: 'Thank you, Sir. That will be £4.50.'

CUSTOMER: '£4.50 for two! You know what you can do with them, don't you?'

SALESMAN: 'Yes, sir ... I'm sorry I cannot oblige you at the moment; I'm dealing with a complaint from a customer over the price of a pineapple ...'

The Duke of Bedford

Once, whilst speaking at a meeting, I was given a doubtful microphone so I asked, 'Can you hear me at the back?' The answer came, 'Yes,' and I replied, 'I am glad, for I was speaking somewhere the other day, and when I asked the same question, a lady at the back said, "No", and one sitting at the front got up and said, "I can – let me change places with you!"'

Lord Moyne, MA, FRSL

I know no after dinner stories, which is perhaps the reason that I have only spoken once after a dinner and was never asked to do so again!

Martin Stevens, JP, MP

A hairdresser and a Member of Parliament arrived in Heaven simultaneously. St Peter handed the MP his bicycle, the key to his council flat and a folder of luncheon vouchers. The new arrival was just moving away, quite contented, when he noticed the hairdresser being shown to his chauffeur-driven Rolls-Royce, into which a case of champagne was being loaded. The title deeds of his country estate were being carried by a secretary and St Peter was pointing out the spacious town house which had been allocated to him. The Member of Parliament said, 'I don't want to complain, but why is that other chap doing so well? After all I *was* an MP.' St Peter replied, 'Heaven is jam-packed with Members of Parliament – but he's the first hairdresser we've ever had.'

Lord Strauss, PC

'Your name?' asked St Peter at the gates of Heaven.

'Mary Smith,' replied the applicant.

'There are many Mary Smiths,' said St Peter. 'Can you identify yourself further? For instance, by your husband's last words. We have a full record of last words.'

'Certainly. They were, "Mary, if you are ever unfaithful to

my memory, I will turn in my grave".'

'Ah,' said St Peter, 'you must be the widow of the man we know as "revolving Smith".'

Major-General The Viscount Monckton of Brenchley, CB, OBE, MC, DL

On his way back from the Commons to his Club in St James's, F.E. Smith (later Lord Birkenhead) always called in at the Athenaeum to use the lavatory. He did this for some months, until somebody asked the Secretary if he was a member and it was discovered that he was not. The next time he arrived at the Club, the Secretary was standing ready to greet him, and asked him if he was a member.

'Oh,' replied F.E. Smith, 'is it also a club?'

Lord Brimelow, GCMG, OBE

Two Poles meet on the street.

'Have you heard the latest news?' asks one. 'The Russians have landed on the moon.'

'What? All of them?'

Lord Mancroft, KBE, TD

Some months ago I was rung up by the Chairman and Secretary of one of the Inns of Court Debating Societies, with which I have long been on friendly terms.

'Lord Mancroft,' they said, 'give us your advice. Do you know the Lord Chancellor, Lord Hailsham?'

11

'Yes, of course,' I said, 'Why?'

'Well,' they replied. 'Tell us quite frankly. Do you think he would be mortally offended if we were to ask him to step in at literally a minute's notice and take the place, at our annual dinner, of our guest of honour who's fallen sick?'

'Now steady on,' I said. 'Lord Hailsham is not only a Senior Cabinet Minister, he is also one of the most sought-after speakers in the country. It depends largely, doesn't it, upon the calibre of your stricken guest of honour. I mean, if you've succeeded in attracting to your table somebody outside the normal run of after-dinner speakers – the Ayahtollah Khomeini, for instance, or Miss Elizabeth Taylor, perhaps *that* might make a difference. Who is it?'

They mentioned the name of a Mr Bert Buggins, or somebody I'd never heard of in my life before.

'Good heavens,' I said, 'you can't do that to somebody of Lord Hailsham's calibre. He'll be mortally offended. Bitterly hurt.'

'Oh Lord Mancroft,' they said, 'how grateful we are to you for speaking so frankly. You've saved us from making fools of ourselves and dropping a dreadful brick.' Then, after a short pause, 'Lord Mancroft, I suppose *you* wouldn't care to come and make the speech for us?'

Martin Stevens, JP, MP

A Central European peasant was granted three wishes in exchange for sparing the life of a frog. He asked for great wealth, royal birth, and a beautiful wife. There was a flash of lightning and he came to, to find himself between silken sheets, in a four-poster bed under a royal coat-of-arms. A lovely girl, in bed beside him, took him into her arms. 'Get a move on, Franz Ferdinand,' she said. 'We are due in Sarajevo in twenty minutes.'

Sir Shuldham Redfern, KCVO, CMG

Some forty years ago, Mr Justice Norman Birkett was the Guest of Honour at a dinner in Toronto given by the Ontario Bar Association. The Chairman was the Canadian judge Mr Justice McCarthy, who introduced Birkett in a long and rather conventional speech. Birkett, one of the greatest of after-dinner speakers, began his reply as follows:

There is a legend among the Irish that when a child is born it is kissed by an angel. If the angel kisses it on its brow it will grow up to have great intellectual qualities. If the angel kisses it on its hands it will soon show unusual manual dexterity. If the angel kisses it on its feet it will become a swift runner and a good athlete. I don't know where the angel kissed Mr Justice McCarthy, but he certainly makes an excellent Chairman.

Sir John Osborn, MP

Quite often on public occasions, I have to explain that my name is John Osborn and that I neither write plays nor books. Frequently John Osborne's correspondence is muddled with mine and since I have entered Parliament we have had to exchange letters with each other on several occasions. But in 1957 I was on a business visit to the United States of America, well before I had given any serious thought to being a Member of Parliament.

My flight left late, and I drove through Broadway to my hotel noticing that *Look Back in Anger* was having its première that week. When I reached my hotel, it did not occur to me that the bellboys, porters and receptionists might be

14

aspiring actors and actresses. As my flight had left late, and as I had arrived after 7 o'clock, I learned to my chagrin that my reservation had been cancelled. I made some wry comment to the effect that this was a fine way to treat an Englishman on a visit to New York, but a sweet girl behind the reception counter said:

'Say, Mr Osborn, did you say you came from England?'

My reply was 'Yes'.

'Did you say your name was John Osborn?'

My reply was 'Yes'.

'Then you must be *the* John Osborne?'

Naturally my reply was 'Yes' – and I got a room immediately.

William Deedes, Editor, *Daily Telegraph*

Hark to the tale of Frederick Worms
Whose parents weren't on speaking terms;
So, when Fred wrote to Santa Claus,
He wrote in duplicate, because
One went to Dad and one to Mum,
Each asking for plutonium.

So Fred's father and his mother,
Without consulting one another,
Each sent a lump of largish size,
Intending it as a surprise.

These met in Frederick's stocking, and
Laid waste some ten square miles of land.
Learn from this tale of nuclear fission,
Not to mix science with superstition!

Lord Porritt, GCMG, GCVO, CBE

A junior Civil Servant went to the office of his senior with important papers and, after knocking and getting no reply, cautiously opened the door to find his Chief standing, with his hands behind his back, looking out of the windows onto Whitehall. The junior felt it wiser to retire quietly – but on being informed of the urgency of the message he carried, he returned an hour later, and again knocked on the door of the Chief's office. Still receiving no reply, he ventured in and cautiously made his presence known.

His Chief turned slowly and said, 'Quite extraordinary, Smithers, but I can now understand why this country doesn't prosper. I have been watching the workmen out there and they haven't done anything for the past hour!'

Neil Marten, PC, MP was conducting a group of his constituents around the Houses of Parliament when he came to a lobby of the House of Lords to be confronted by the Lord Chancellor, Viscount Hailsham, in all his regalia. The Chancellor immediately recognised him and called out, 'Neil!', and with that, the constituents – misinterpreting the call – fell down upon their knees.

Ian Lang, MP

A certain Scottish Labour MP, not noted for his assiduous attendance at the House of Commons, also had the reputation of being difficult to contact at home.

On one occasion, a Parliamentary colleague telephoned

17

him, to be greeted with:

'Hello, this is a recording. I am out at present on constituency business. Would you please leave your message after the tone and I will attend to it as soon as possible. Pip! Pip! Pip!'

'Hello. This is your Party Whip speaking. I wanted to let you know that there is an important vote in the House on a three-line whip, on Tuesday night, so I hope you will be there to support the party.'

'Oh, it's you, Hugh! Why didn't you say so? What can I do for you?'

Mrs Lynda Chalker, MP

So often one hears today that 'lack of communication' is the cause of the lack of understanding between those 'in authority' and those subject to such authority; e.g. that the clergy have nothing in common with those to whom they preach, and the politicians have nothing in common with those whom they punish.

I received a telephone call one day from the deputy governor of a prison, where I was a visiting magistrate, which stated that one of the prisoners had a complaint to make and insisted on seeing me. I duly visited the prison and listened to the complaint which the prisoner was making on behalf of himself and several others. I told him that whilst I considered the complaint to be serious and justified, I could not understand why he could not have waited until the next regular call of the visiting magistrate nor why he had insisted upon seeing me in particular.

He replied that he had discussed the matter with his fellow prisoners, and they all felt that the complaint should be made to me personally. I said that this was what I could not understand – why to me?

To this question he replied, in all seriousness, that they all took the view that their complaint would receive much greater consideration from me because, he said, 'we all think you are so much like one of us.'

I like to think that this was meant as a tribute. Or was it?

David Mellor, MP

A missionary was walking along a jungle path in Africa one day when he suddenly came face to face with a lion. Fearing that his last moments had come, the missionary fell to his knees and covered his face with his hands.

Seconds, it seemed almost like minutes, ticked away and nothing happened, and hope began to dawn in the missionary's breast. Gingerly, he pulled aside his fingers and peeped through. He was startled to see the lion, similarly on his knees with his paws covering his eyes.

The hope that had begun to dawn, swelled, and became real optimism. Then the lion pulled his paws aside, stared at the missionary and said, 'I don't know about you, mate, but I'm saying grace!'

Robert Rhodes James, MP

A favourite story of mine which used to be told by Mr Kruschev.

One freezing day in the Ukraine, there was a little boy walking through the woods, whistling. Suddenly, he saw a small bird with a broken wing, being chased by a hungry fox. The little boy picked up the bird, comforted it, and then looked for a warm and comfortable place where it could recover. At that moment, along came a horse and left a large deposit on the road. The little boy scooped a hole in the

deposit, put the little bird in it, and went away, whistling.

He was quite right. In the warm environment of the dung the little bird recovered, and put out his head and sang for joy. The hungry fox heard it, and ate the little bird.

The moral of this story is twofold: First, it is not always your enemies who put you in it, and secondly, if you are in it up to your neck, keep your mouth shut!

There is a moral here for all politicians!

Julian Amery, PC, MP

This story is based on a visit to the Military Hospital in Singapore by the Secretary of State for War. The setting is a ward with three corporals in it.

SECRETARY OF STATE FOR WAR: 'Corporal Tomkins, what's the matter with you?'

CORPORAL TOMKINS:'VD, Sir.'

SEC. OF STATE FOR WAR: 'I am sorry about that. Wouldn't have expected it from a non-commissioned officer with your experience. What's the cure?'

TOMKINS: 'They gives me a brush, they gives me some ointment and they tells me to paint the affected part.'

SEC. OF STATE FOR WAR: 'What's your ambition?'

TOMKINS: 'Get well, so I can go back to Malaya and kill some terrorists.'

SEC. OF STATE FOR WAR: 'Good man.'

The Secretary of State for War then moves to the next bed and remarks:

'Corporal Smith, what's the matter with you?'

CORPORAL SMITH: 'Piles, Sir.'

SEC. OF STATE FOR WAR: 'I believe it's very distressing.'

SMITH: 'Yes Sir, very distressing.'

SEC. OF STATE FOR WAR: 'What's the treatment?'

SMITH: 'They gives me a brush, they gives me some ointment, and tells me to paint the affected part.'

SEC. OF STATE FOR WAR: 'What's your ambition?'

SMITH: 'Get well, Sir, and get back to the Regiment as soon as possible.'

SEC. OF STATE FOR WAR: 'Good man.'

The Secretary of State for War goes to the next bed and asks: 'Corporal Brown, what's the matter with you?'

CORPORAL BROWN, (faintly): 'Laryngitis.'

SEC. OF STATE FOR WAR: 'What did you say?'

BROWN: 'Laryngitis, Sir.'

SEC. OF STATE FOR WAR: 'Very tiresome for you. What's the treatment?'

BROWN: 'They gives me a brush, they gives me some ointment, and they tells me to paint the affected part.'

SEC. OF STATE FOR WAR: 'What's your ambition?'

BROWN: 'To get the brush before the other two.'

John Carlisle, MP

On the occasion before the England *v* Wales rugby match at Twickenham, I made two requests to one Speaker. The first was for an Adjournment Debate later that week, and the second for tickets for the match. His reply was as follows:

'The first request is within my power and I can accommodate, the second, however, is beyond my jurisdiction, but I can assure you of one thing: if England beats Wales at Twickenham on Saturday, you will not be called to speak before Easter!'

John Corrie, MP

An old lady who was lonely bought two parrots. She was not

sure which was male and which was female.

'Ah,' said the pet shop owner, 'it's easy to tell the difference. Parrots make love every morning: the answer is to cover the cage, creep in first thing, and whip off the cover; you can pick out the male bird as he always shuts his eyes and has a rest.'

The old lady did this and, sure enough, was able to pick out the male, but to ensure that she knew him in future she cut out a little white collar and put it round his neck.

All went well until two weeks later when the Vicar called to tea. The male parrot looked up, saw him and squawked, 'Tough luck, you were caught at it as well, I see!'

Toby Jessel, MP

A man who thought he was a dog was sent to a psychiatrist who said, 'This is very serious – we had better have a talk about this. Please go over there, lie down on that sofa and relax; to which the man replied, 'Sorry, but I am not allowed on sofas.'

Lord Porrit, PC, GCMG, GCVO, CBE

A junior Civil Servant found a 'Top Secret' document on his desk, read it, initialled it and sent it out to his Chief. The latter, furious at this presumption on his junior's part, called him in and dressed him down, saying, 'You will delete your initials and initial the deletion!'

John Lee, MP

In 1975 the Nelson and Colne Constituency Conservative Association's Selection Committee were interviewing possible candidates to take on the sitting Labour Member of Parliament, Douglas Hoyle, at the General Election.

One question to a young aspirant from the South of England was put by a Selection Committee member with a strong Lancashire accent: 'What are you going to do about Doug 'oyle?'

The aspiring candidate, nervously fingering his tie and looking for guidance from the Chairman, said, 'I ... I wasn't sure there *was* any oil in this constituency.'

Percy Grieve, QC, MP

From a platform in Hyde Park, at Speaker's Corner, a left-wing agitator was haranguing the crowd on the benefits to be derived from full-blooded Socialism. 'When the dawn of freedom comes,' he said, turning to a little man in a cloth cap on the edge of the crowd, 'you will be riding down Park Lane in a Rolls-Royce car, with a top hat on your head.'

'Beg pardon, Guv,' said the little man, 'I couldn't see meself in a top 'at. I'd rather stick to me old titfer.'

'Very well, then,' said the orator. 'When the dawn of freedom comes, my friend, you will be riding down Park Lane in a Rolls-Royce car, wearing you own old titfer.'

'Beg pardon, Guv.' said the little man. 'Couldn't really see meself in a Rolls-Royce. Think I'd be far better on me old bike.'

'Look here,' said the orator. 'When the dawn of freedom comes, you'll do what you're bloody well told.'

Michael Jopling, PC, MP

A Member of Parliament was giving prizes away at a Girls' School's Speech Day. Afterwards the Head Mistress asked how much he wanted to cover his expenses, which he naturally refused. To this, the Head Mistress replied: 'Oh! That is generous. It will allow us to put the money we had for your expenses into a special fund we have.'

The MP did not like to ask what the special little fund was for but, in the end, his curiosity got the better of his good manners, and he did ask. The Head Mistress replied: 'Oh! It is a special little fund so that we can afford a rather better speaker next year!'

Malcolm Rifkind, MP

In the 1930s there was an old Scots Provost of a small burgh in Scotland, who, having been recently elected to his office, had to preside over his first civic banquet. He was told that his first responsibility would be to propose the Loyal Toast to His Majesty King George V. Having never had to give such a Toast before, nor having heard one proposed, the Provost spent many days preparing a lengthy speech extolling the many virtues of His Majesty, which he intended to use in the Toast he was to make.

Fortunately, he showed the proposed lengthy speech to the Town Clerk, who was aghast at the kind of speech that had been prepared and who informed the Provost that when one was proposing the Loyal Toast, one was merely expected to propose the health of His Majesty and then sit down.

The Provost was somewhat annoyed and disconcerted at this advice, but he felt that he had no alternative but to accept it. Accordingly, on the night in question, at the appropriate time he rose and addressed the assembled guests in the following fashion: 'Ladies and Gentlemen, I wish to propose the Toast to His Majesty King George V and the Town Clerk tells me the less I say about him the better!'

Stephen Hastings, MC, MP

A surgeon, an anaesthetist, an architect and a politician were discussing which of their professions was the most ancient. The surgeon claimed that it must be his since the resection of Adam's rib was well documented and constituted a major operation. The anaesthetist said that if that was so, then there was no doubt that a deep sleep had been necessary beforehand and that therefore his practice preceded the surgeon's. 'Maybe,' said the architect, 'but before all that happened, it was the task of the architect of the universe to arrange the stars in their courses and to produce order from chaos.'

The politician looked knowingly at the three of them and said, 'And who do you suppose created the chaos?'

Sir Anthony Royle, KCMG, MP

This story is about a knight who returned to his castle late in the evening in a state of total disarray, with dented armour, his face bleeding, his horse crippled, and the knight himself about to fall off the limping animal.

'What has befallen you, goodly knight?' asked the lord of the castle.

'Sire, I have been working for you, robbing, raping and pillaging your enemies in the West.'

27

'You have what?' cried the lord. 'I do not have any enemies in the West.'

'Oh,' said the knight. 'I think you do now.'

Lord Glendevon, PC

Two horses met when out for a walk, and one said to the other 'I know your pace but I can't put a mane to it.'

Lord Renton, PC, KBE, TD, QC

Dr W.G. Grace had a son who was a master at Oundle. When they were both invited to play cricket for the Masters against the 1st XI hundreds of people came to see the great man play, and when he went in to bat there was tremendous applause. The school fast bowler, however, bowled him out first ball – and an awful groan was heard all round the ground.

On his way back to the pavilion WG said to the boy: 'Young man! You see all those people – they didn't come here to see you bowl!'

Lord McFadzean, KT

There was a teetotal preacher who once ended his vigorous sermon with the plea that: 'All liquor should be thrown into the river', only to go on and announce as the last hymn: 'Shall we gather at the river'!

Sir Hugh Fraser, PC, MBE, MP

A young Minister was sent to Moscow and found whilst he was there that he had to attend a dinner and thereafter make a speech. He decided to surprise everyone by making the speech in Russian.

He set about learning his speech but, since time was short, he could only learn the Russian phonetically.

The speech he had prepared was a short one but as he was on his way to make it, he realised that he did not know how to say 'Ladies and Gentlemen'. He stopped the car and looked about him and there, in front of him, was the very public place he was looking for. He set off once again for the dinner.

As he started to speak in Russian he found that he did not get the delighted applause he had expected – more a deathly silence. The rest of the speech seemed to go better and he did receive a polite appreciation at the end of it.

Afterwards he asked one of his colleagues what had gone wrong. The colleague replied: 'The speech was excellent. It might just have been that you started off "Male and female urinals"!'

Reg Prentice, PC, JP, MP

Many reasons have been given by people as to why they should have crossed the floor from one political party to another (I should know!), but this story gives one that is slightly unorthodox:

Tom and Harry had been active Conservatives for many years, working together in the same branch. When Tom was taken ill, Harry visited him and was astonished to hear the statement, 'I have just decided to join the Labour Party.'

'For goodness' sake, why?' asked Harry. 'You have been a "True Blue" Tory all your life. Why change now?'

'Well, I am not feeling at all well. I do not like the way the doctor is looking at me. I feel I may not have long to live. And if someone is going to die, I would rather it was one of those so-and-sos, not one of us!'

Robin Leigh-Pemberton, Chairman, National Westminster Bank Ltd, FRSA, CBIM

A well-to-do country lady formed the ambition to establish a fine pedigree herd of beef cattle. Local opinion, including that of the Ministry of Agriculture, doubted her ability to do this and she was well aware of these doubts. When the herd had been assembled, she invited the Ministry Officer to come and inspect it, and he was compelled to admit that it was indeed a very fine herd. 'But,' he continued, 'if I had a herd of thirty head, I would have twenty-nine cows and one bull and not, like you, fifteen cows and fifteen bulls.'

'Yes, I know,' she replied, 'but that's a man's point of view.'

Baroness Hornsby-Smith, PC, DBE, FRSA

When Under-Secretary of State at the Home Office, I was due to visit Remand Homes and Borstals in the West Country. I was met at Exeter by a police car to complete my cross-country schedule. On proceeding to Plymouth, I was met by the Chief Constable in his car and he led the way to what had been an old mansion. On parade and gazing through the French windows were thirty 'naughty' girls.

The Chief Constable leapt out of his car and joined me,

while my police driver opened the door and the girls goggled. That it might be courtesy never entered their heads – it could only be *custody* – an awe-struck voice uttered: 'Cor blimey, she must be an 'ot one – 2 police cars and 3 cops to bring 'er in.'

Sir John Tilney, Kt, TD, JP Chairman, Airey Neave Memorial Trust

I like shorter stories, the shorter the quip the better. For instance, the story of the prisoner in the dock who said after being sentenced, 'Me Lud, I swear I am innocent, but I will never do it again!'

Lord Beswick, PC

The motivating power of professional pride should not be under-estimated. Consider for example the following case.

A Corporation in a certain totalitarian country was adjudged by the appropriate court to have failed the nation. The Chairman, Finance Director, and Engineering Director, were each sentenced to death by guillotine.

On the appointed day, before a great crowd, the Chairman put his head on the block and the lever was pulled, but the blade did not fall. The law of the land forbade a second try and the Chairman walked away a free man.

The Finance Director went next. Again the lever was pulled, and again, the blade failed to fall and the Finance Director also was freed.

Then came their remaining colleague. The Engineering Director put his head upon the block; as the lever was about

32

to be pulled he looked up and called out, 'Wait a minute. I can see what's wrong.'

Hugh Cubbitt, CBE, FRICS, JP, DL, FRSA

A newspaper editor wrote a swingeingly critical article about his local council in which he claimed that '... half the Councillors are crooks ...' After strong remonstrance and threat of libel action, he amended on publication to '... half the Councillors are *not* crooks....'

The Duke of Norfolk, CB, CBE, MC, DL

I have often found it hard to explain who I am when answering the telephone, and on one occasion, having said, on lifting up the receiver, 'Duke of Norfolk', I got the spontaneous reponse: 'What's that, a pub?'

Sir Shuldham Redfern, KCVO, CMG

A firm of insurance brokers put up a new and very modern office building in the City and wanted to have on the outside five plaques, each of which would represent some aspect of insurance. They therefore sent for Epstein, explained what they wanted and left it to him to submit drawings of appropriate designs.

In due course the drawings arrived. The first was of a man in bed with his wife, the second of a man in bed with his fiancée, the third of a man in bed with his secretary, the fourth of a man in bed with a lady of easy virtue and the fifth

33

of a man in bed alone. When they saw these drawings the members of the Board were furious. They sent for Epstein and said that there must be some misunderstanding, for not one of these drawings appeared to have anything to do with insurance.

'On the contrary', said Epstein. 'Each of these drawings does, as you requested, represent some aspect of insurance. For instance, the first, of a man and wife, is Legal and General. The second, of a man and his fiancée, is Mutual Trust. The third, of a man and his secretary, is Employer's Liability, and the fourth, of a man and a lady of easy virtue, is Commercial Union.'

'What about the fifth, a man alone?' said the Managing Director.

'Oh that,' said Epstein, 'is obviously Prudential.'

Lord Blake, FBA, JP

The Chairman of a meeting, as Chairmen sometimes do, introduced the guest speaker at inordinate length, reciting all major and most minor details of his career. At last he finished and said, 'I will now ask Lord Birkenhead to give his Address.' Lord Birkenhead replied, '32 Grosvenor Gardens, SW1,' and walked out of the hall.

Tom Benyon, MP

A man rang his local District Council and spoke to the Ratings Officer.

'How much extra do I pay for building a stable block, a huge barn and a greenhouse?'

'£400 p.a. extra.'

'Excellent, I have just pulled them down!'

Barry Henderson, MP

Having rescued a mongrel from the Cat and Dog Home we found we were often asked her breed. At first we didn't like to be too crudely direct about her very mixed ancestry.

As she was called Sheba, for a day or two we had been answering the usual question by calling her an 'Ethiopian Moon Hound', until my wife giving this answer at a cocktail party got the reply, 'That's interesting, we were in Ethiopia last month and didn't see any of them.'

Next week I was in Dundee and a large and cheerful lady, enchanted by the dog, asked the usual question, to which I replied 'I'm afraid she is quite unique.' She said, 'A euneekie, I havna come across one of them afore.'

We no longer bother with euphemisms!

The Earl of Waldegrave,
KG, GCVO, TD, DL

Q. Name a well known husband and wife in the Bible?
A. Dan and Beersheba.
Q. No.
A. I forgot, Sir ... of course, they weren't properly married ... what about Sodom and Gomorrah?

Sir James Hanson, Kt

The difference between political beliefs:
SOCIALISM: You have two cows, and you give one to your neighbour.

COMMUNISM: You have two cows, the government takes both of them and gives you the milk.

BUREAUCRACY: You have two cows, the government takes both of them, shoots one of them, milks the other and pours the milk down the drain.

CAPITALISM: You have two cows, you sell one of them and buy a bull.

The Viscount Trenchard, MC

'I can clearly discern a light at the end of the tunnel.'

Private Secretary: 'Are you sure, Sir, that it's not an engine coming the other way?'

Lord Home of the Hirsel, PC, KT

A man who was losing his memory consulted a specialist.

SPECIALIST: 'When did this begin?'
PATIENT: 'When did what begin?'

Lord Stuart

The elephant looked at the mouse and said, 'Why are you so small?' The mouse replied, 'Oh, dear, I have not been very well recently.'

Lord Harmar-Nicholls, MEP, JP

A mother flea giving guidance on Life to her three daughters said, 'Always have a worthy watchword and adhere to it. Mine has always been "perserverance".

'When I was a young and beautiful flea like you are now, I lived on a church hassock. One day I heard that an Archbishop was coming to our church and I made up my mind that I would taste the Archbishop.

'On the great day I hid in the porch and when he arrived I jumped on his hand, but he brushed me off. I persevered and followed him down the aisle and jumped on his neck, again he brushed me off. Still I persevered and followed him to the altar and jumped behind his ear, and it was there, my children, that, as a result of my perseverance, I tasted my first Archbishop; but what is more, it was there that I met your dear father.'

Ivan Lawrence, QC, MP

I once attended a meeting where the Toastmaster announced the main speaker thus:

'My Lords, Ladies and Gentlemen, pray for the silence of your Member of Parliament.'

Lord Carr of Hadley, PC, CH

An ageing Bishop found himself increasingly unable to cease from wondering whether there were any golf courses in Heaven. He even put the question into his prayers.

One day, while meditating, he received a direct message

from above: 'Don't worry,' the Heavenly messenger said. 'There are plenty of the most wonderful golf courses, they are always in perfect condition, and never have any wind or rain to put you off your game, and, of course, there is a great choice of the nicest people to play with.'

'Oh, that is wonderful news,' said the Bishop.

'Yes,' replied the messenger, 'but now for the bad news. You are down to play in a match on Saturday!'

Lord Duncan-Sandys, PC, CH

I am told that the Dean of Windsor once asked King George V what he would like him to preach about on Sunday, to which the King replied, 'About ten minutes.'

D.R.W. Silk, JP, MA, The Warden, Radley College

A Bishop was struggling through a Series 3 service with a microphone which seemed not to be working. He turned to the Dean who was beside him, and, tapping the microphone, he whispered to the Dean, 'There is something wrong with this thing.' Back came the instant response of the large congregation, 'And also with you.'

The Viscount Rochdale, OBE, TD, DL

An eminent writer of prose and poetry had become very run down, so he went to his doctor to ask what he should do. The doctor immediately told him to go away into the country for a while, for a change and rest.

He followed the doctor's advice and went to a little

country hotel. When the time came for him to leave, the landlord realised that to have something written personally in his Visitors Book by such an eminent writer would be a great boost. He therefore asked his guest if he would write something. The latter was rather irritated, but eventually was persuaded to contribute, and this he did as follows:

'My doctor sent me here for a change and rest,

The waiter took the change and the landlord took the rest!

The Hon. William Waldegrave, MP

Two lunatics visit the House of Commons.

They watch happily as Members boo, shout and catcall. They feel more and more at home as order papers are waved, and old gentlemen in knee breeches and swords lead away the Member for Boltover.

Suddenly a bell rings, and everyone scurries away into the lobbies. 'Ah,' says one lunatic to the other, 'someone has escaped.'

Lord Caccia, GCMG, GCVO

There are many tales ascribed to Nasrudin in the Near and Middle East. One, recorded amongst others, in the *Pleasantries of the Incredible Mullah*, describes how he stood up in the market place and started to address the throng.

'O people! Do you want knowledge without difficulties, truth without falsehood, attainment without effort, progress without sacrifice?'

Very soon a large crowd gathered; everyone shouting, 'Yes, yes.'

'Excellent,' said the Mullah, 'I only wanted to know. You may rely upon me to tell you all about it, if I ever discover any such thing.'

J. Allan Stewart, MP

There are countless stories about the attitude of the English to the Scots and vice-versa. My favourite concerns an election meeting in England where the speaker was being mercilessly heckled by an immigrant from north of the border.

Stung by the remarks about his integrity and patriotism, the speaker began his peroration, 'Mr Chairman, I am an Englishman, I have always been proud to be an Englishman, and I venture to suggest I always shall be proud to be an Englishman.'

'Man, man,' came the sorrowful question, 'dae ye huv nae ambition at all?'

Eamon Kennedy, Ambassador, Irish Embassy

Diplomats know that the timing of their démarches is all-important. It is said that when Machiavelli was on his deathbed he was visited by a humble priest who wished to offer the last rites.

'Wake up, Machiavelli,' he said, 'I'm here to give you the last rites. Tell me – do you renounce the devil?'

Machiavelli's eyes were open now and he peered at the holy man.

'Do you renounce the devil?' asked the priest again.

'Renounce him?' replied Machiavelli. 'Surely you don't really think this would be the right time to antagonise him?'

42

The Viscount Norwich, FRSL

James McNeill Whistler commissioned a house – the White House, Chelsea – from his architect friend, E.W. Godwin. Some years later, when Whistler was compelled by poverty to leave the house, he put up a plaque over the door. It read: 'Except the Lord build the house, their labour is but lost that build it. E.W. Godwin, FSA, built this one.'

Sir Kenneth Lewis, DL, MP

Moses went up the mountain to negotiate The Commandments with the Lord on behalf of the children of Israel.

But Moses first discussed with the shop stewards at the bottom of the mountain, everything which, it was thought, the Lord might require in the Commandments.

Moses returned after some time and said he had done his best to get a deal.

Moses said, 'The Lord wanted fifteen commandments – I tried to get this reduced to eight – so, we settled on ten and I am sorry to have to report that number seven (about adultery) which you Comrades wanted out, has had to stay in!'

Lord McFadzean, KT

An opening when one has been rather forced to make a speech:

43

'As I stand up to speak I am vividly reminded of the man who built himself a grand house with an ultra-large swimming pool. Having invited many friends to a big party round the swimming pool and plied them with drinks, he then invited any of them to swim in the pool, notifying them that there was a live alligator in it but that anyone who did go in and get out safely could have half his estate or the hand of his younger daughter in marriage.

Naturally, nothing much happened until one man was seen swimming madly for the steps hotly pursued by the alligator. When he had reached safety, the host, in congratulating him, asked him which of his offers he wanted: half his property or the hand of his younger daughter in marriage.

'Neither,' spluttered the swimmer furiously. 'I only want one thing and that is to find the b——r who shoved me in.'

An opening sentence, when one feels totally inadequate for the particular occasion:

The story of the two cows munching contentedly in a meadow when down the adjacent country lane came an ultra-modern milk tanker with the words protruding from its gleaming cylinder, 'This milk is Standardised, Pasteurised and Homogenised with Vitamin D added.' Said one cow to another while shaking its head sadly: 'It does make you feel so totally inadequate.'

An appropriate story in an overseas country, when there are foreigners there who do understand English fairly well and you are going to give part of your speech in the language of the country you are in. Drift in to such part of your speech with due apologies and the memory of the foreigner who was trying desperately to impress his British audience with his knowledge of English and said: 'You think I know damned nothing but I can assure you I know damned all.'

45

Lord Simon of Glaisdale, PC, DL

At a recent dinner my name appeared next on the toast list. The Chairman rose and said, 'I now call on our little northern nightingale.' I was a little surprised, but then I'd failed to notice a musical interlude. Just as I was opening my mouth, a soprano, who'd taken her place at my elbow, burst into song. When she had finished the Chairman rose again and said, 'That concludes the part of the evening devoted to your entertainment – I now call on Mr Simon.'

Sir Anthony Royle, KCMG, MP

Boring speakers remind one of the famous old politician who having talked interminably and boringly about himself, turned to his companion and said, 'I have talked about myself long enough. Let's talk about you. What do you think of me?'

Sir Monty Finniston, Kt, BSc, PhD, FRS, FRSE

'Lord, thank you for the food we are about to eat, and for the company gathered here this evening, all of whom hold responsible positions in industry and commerce. Guide us in our actions and decisions in that they are taken in the best interests of those for whom we are responsible and not purely for the advancement of ourselves as individuals. When it comes to my time to speak, Lord, fill my mouth with worthwhile stuff and nudge me when I have said enough.'

46

Lord Wade, DL, MA, LLB

Chairman: We are very grateful to Lord Wade for coming to speak to us at such short notice. I can assure him that we would have been very willing to make do with a less distinguished speaker, but we couldn't find one!

The Viscount Mountgarret

A man who was a good friend of an eminent member of the Royal Yacht Squadron was invited to give a post prandial talk at the Squadron's Annual Dinner. The Dinner was for men only, and when the time came for the speech to be made, the man rose to his feet and said, 'Gentlemen, it is a very great honour to be invited to speak to you this evening, but I am at a loss to know exactly what to talk to you about. It is pointless my talking to you about matters concerning sailing, as I am not half as experienced as all of you, but I do know a considerable amount about sex – and I propose to speak to you about that.' And so he did.

The following morning his wife was up at her usual punctual hour, with her husband still sleeping off the effects of a rather jovial evening the night before. Outside, she happened to meet somebody who had been at the dinner. 'Oh,' she said, 'I'm so delighted to see you – I've been dying to know how Willie got on last night. I was sound asleep when he got back, and he hasn't surfaced yet. Do tell me what happened.'

'Oh,' her acquaintance replied, 'he was an absolutely roaring success. He was frightfully funny, and we all thoroughly enjoyed ourselves.'

'Oh, I'm so glad,' she said, 'you see I was terribly worried about him. He's only done it three times. The first time he was violently sick. The second time his hat blew off, and the third time he got all tangled up in the sheets!'

Lord Maybray-King, PC, DCL, PhD, FKC

At a meeting the speaker started by saying, 'I'm going to talk to you about Yale University – Y-A-L-E – Yale: Y for Youth, A for Ambition, L for Loyalty and E for Endeavour'; and he spoke for half an hour on each.

He later said to a friend, 'Did you like my speech?'

'Yes,' came the reply, 'but it's a good job it wasn't on the Massachusetts Institute of Technology!'

The Hon. Peter Brooke, MP

Letter from a schoolgirl,
'Dear Aunt,
The school did *Hamlet* last week. Most of the parents had seen it before, but they laughed just the same.'

The Hon. Archie Hamilton, MP

I am always rather touched by the story of the speaker who finds himself in much the same position as the third husband-to-be of Brigitte Bardot, a man some years younger than his would-be bride. He was asked how he viewed his forthcoming marriage, and replied, 'I know what I am supposed to do, but it is a question of how to make it more interesting.'

49

Tom Benyon, MP

A man went to stay at a hotel in Workington. On the second day he rang room service: 'Please send me some tepid coffee, some soggy toast, a raw egg and some warm orange juice.'

'Sir, I am afraid we don't provide that sort of breakfast, we are a 4-star Hotel.'

'Why not? You did yesterday!'

Lord Maybray-King, PC, DCL, PhD, FKC

A man died and went to Heaven. He knocked at the door and it was opened by Satan. The man was astonished. 'Don't worry,' said Satan. 'We've gone comprehensive.'

Lord Lloyd of Dolobran, MBE, DL

A bishop who was not renowned for the brevity of his sermons, visited one of the churches in his Diocese. When he arrived, he was not best pleased to find a total congregation of about ten people including the choir.

After the service was over, he said to the Vicar, 'That was a very small congregation we had this evening, did you not tell your parishioners that I was coming?'

'No,' said the Vicar, 'but I'm afraid that it must have leaked out!'

51

Sir Shuldham Redfern, KCVO, CMG

A Bishop was once giving a lecture to a class of small boys on the subject of Moral Courage. At the end of the lecture he said: 'Now can any boy give me a good example of Moral Courage?' A boy put up his hand and said: 'Yes, Sir, I can. There were twelve boys in a dormitory and when they went to bed eleven of them undressed and jumped into bed, but one of them knelt down and said his prayers first. That showed Moral Courage.'

'A very good example,' said the Bishop. 'Can you give me another example?'

The same little boy put up his hand and said he could give another example. 'If there were a dormitory in which there were twelve Bishops, and, when they went to bed eleven of them knelt down and said their prayers but the twelfth jumped into bed without saying his prayers, *that* would also be an example of Moral Courage.'

Humphrey Atkins, PC, MP

Paddy and Sean are bringing a home-made bomb into the city centre in order to leave it outside the post-office.

SEAN, who is holding the bomb on his knee: 'For the Blessed Mary's sake, Paddy, drive a little slower – this bomb might go off at any minute!'

PADDY: 'Sure, and it doesn't matter if it does, we've got a spare one in the boot!'

John Heddle, MP

Sir Thomas Beecham was travelling south, having conducted the Hallé Orchestra, in a first-class non-smoking compartment (before the days of railway nationalisation). At Stockport he was joined by a buxom lady who promptly lit up a cigarette.

She asked Sir Thomas Beecham: 'I hope you don't mind if I smoke,' to which the great composer replied, 'Not if you don't mind my being sick!'

'Sir,' she replied, 'I'll have you know that I am one of the directors' wives,' to which Sr TB replied 'Madam, I don't mind if you are the director's *only* wife!'

Eamon Kennedy, Ambassador, Irish Embassy

There was a charming old Irishman living out his last days in a home for the aged in Dublin. To the delight and curiosity of the nurses he seemed to spend every last moment learning the lovely old Gaelic language.

'And why are you spending every moment learning the Irish?' they asked him wonderingly.

'Well, it's because when I go to Heaven all the saints will surely be talking the Gaelic,' he said.

'Well now,' said one of the nurses in fun, 'aren't you the presumptuous old man! Supposing you didn't go up? Supposing you went down, the other way?'

'Not to worry,' said the old man serenely. 'Sure, haven't I got the grand store of English!'

53

Field-Marshal Lord Harding of Petherton, GCB, CBE, DSO, MC

I was complaining to an old fellow West Countryman about having to make after dinner speeches for which, unlike another field-marshal, now sadly deceased, I have little liking and less aptitude. He gave me the following advice: 'Get out of it if you possibly can. If you can't, then stand up straight, speak out loud, and sit down quick!

Sir Kenneth Lewis, DL, MP

A doctor said to his patient who had been back many times, 'I confess, I do not know what is the matter with you, you must have Alice.'

'What's Alice?' asked the patient.

'I don't know,' said the doctor, 'but Christopher Robin went down with it.'

Michael Colvin, MP

The Vicar was having a bad cricket season. He was a member of the team because the cricket field was Church property. All efforts to drop him for this key match were to no avail. His record for the season was dreadful: batting average 3, bowling average infinity and, luckily, no-one kept a tally of the boundaries let through, or the catches dropped.

The Captain placed him at long-on, knowing that the visiting team's opening pair were a stodgy couple and that

the Vicar would be safely out of the way on the boundary behind the bowler.

Alas, contrary to all expectations, the batsman opened his shoulders to the first ball and sent it high into the air over the bowler's head; almost certainly a boundary.

The Vicar was off like lightning. Dashing down the boundary, he flung himself full length and caught the ball six inches from the ground with one hand.

The spectators roared; the Vicar tossed the ball into the air, caught it, rolled over, and the crowd roared with laughter. He bounced it off his nose, and tossed it in the air again. Then, suddenly, hearing the sound of pounding feet, he looked up to see the bowler thundering towards him.

'Throw it in, you bloody fool,' he shouted. 'It was a no-ball, and they've already run eight!'

Lord Maybray-King, PC, DCL, PhD, FKC

Three young Americans were asked who they would like to meet in the next world.

The first said: 'Abraham Lincoln, the greatest of all Americans.'

The second said: 'Robert E. Lee, the noble General of the South.'

The third one was then asked who he would like to meet and he said: 'Brigitte Bardot.'

'But, she's not dead.'

'Neither am I!'

Peter Viggers, MP

Her Brittanic Majesty's Ambassador to Washington was

telephoned by an American he had met at a diplomatic reception. 'I'm telephoning to ask what you would like for Christmas,' said the American.

The Ambassador was embarrassed. He had only met the American once, knew him to be a hugely rich newspaper tycoon, and felt it quite wrong to accept a present from him. He politely demurred, 'Nothing at all, really nothing.'

The American persisted, 'I will be deeply disappointed if you won't tell me. Just name what you are hoping for at Christmas.'

The Ambassador thought quickly. The best way out of the predicament appeared to be a diplomatic compromise: 'Well, if you insist, perhaps a small box of crystallised fruit ... that would be very nice ... thank you very much.'

The Ambassador thought nothing more of the matter until a few weeks later, shortly before Christmas,m a member of his staff silently entered the Ambassador's room, laid an item on the desk and tactfully withdrew.

The item was a newspaper cutting from one of the journals owned by the American. It read: 'At this time of goodwill we have asked the official representatives of other nations to express their wishes for Christmas and the New Year. The French Ambassador hopes for progress towards disarmament through the Strategic Arms Limitation Talks; the German Ambassador hopes that the Brandt Commission Report will lead to the relief of poverty in the Third World ... and the British Ambassador hopes for a small box of crystallised fruit.'

Lord Hooson, QC

An irate female member of an audience suddenly shrieked at Lloyd George: 'If I was your wife I would give you poison,' to which the great man immediately replied, with excessive courtesy, 'Madam, had I the extreme misfortune to be your husband, I'd take it.'

Lord Wolfenden, Kt, CBE

Some years after the end of the Second World War Winston Churchill was enjoying a relaxed evening with a group of intimate friends. One of them pointed out the paradox that the countries which had lost the war, Germany and Japan, were the most prosperous in the world, while the victors, Britain and the United States, seemed to be in an increasingly poor state. 'And what,' enquired Churchill, 'do you propose we should do about it?'

'Well,' said another mischievously, 'we might fight another war and lose it.' Long pause.

'Um,' said the Old Man, 'and whom do you propose we should fight it against?'

'I thought,' came the reply, 'that we might declare war on the United States.' Longer pause.

'Um, well,' rumbled the Great Leader. 'Yes, but, you see, we wouldn't lose.'

Lord Boyd-Carpenter, PC, DL

This is a true story and relates to my grandfather, the late Doctor William Boyd-Carpenter, Bishop of Ripon and Clerk of the Closet to Queen Victoria.

He was summoned one day to Windsor to advise the Queen. It had been discovered that the cobbler who repaired the shoes of the Royal Household at Windsor was an atheist. The question was whether, this having been discovered, he could retain his job.

'Well,' said my grandfather, 'Your Majesty can hardly expect a cobbler to believe in the immortality of the soul.' There was a pause during which it looked as if it was not only the cobbler's job which was in jeopardy. Then the Great Lady gave a hearty laugh and two competent professionals retained their employment.

Lord Orr-Ewing, OBE

When I started in the political field and I was nursing a constituency, I took every opportunity of accepting invitations to speak. I received one from a lunatic asylum and, with some trepidation, accepted it as I felt it would be good practice.

After I had been going for three minutes, a man at the back stood up and shouted: 'Rotten.' I took another run at the sentence with the same result, and when it happened the third time I turned to the Governor of the asylum, who was by my side, and said: 'Shall I go on?'

He replied: 'Do go on. We have had this man here for twenty years and it is the first time I have heard him talk any sense at all!'

Basil de Ferranti, MEP

One evening, having made a speech, a young man came up to the rostrum and said, within everybody's hearing, that mine was the lousiest speech that he had ever heard. The Chairman of the meeting, seeking to defuse the situation, made matters worse by turning to me and saying, 'Oh, Mr de Ferranti, you mustn't mind that young man. All he ever does is to repeat what everyone else is saying.'

59

Leslie Porter, Chairman, Tesco Stores (Holdings) Ltd

Just after the last World War two German ex-officers decided to go to Paris for the weekend. They knew that very attractive ladies gathered during the cocktail hour at the George V Hotel, and thus headed straight there. They agreed that they would only speak English, for fear of ruining their chances.

They entered the lounge of the hotel, called the waiter over and in beautiful English one said: 'Two Martinis, please, waiter.' 'Dry?' asked the waiter, to which one of them immediately answered: 'Nein, zwei.'

Lord Balfour of Inchrye, PC, MC

There was a Bishop of portly dimensions who was very conscious of the dignity of his office. Whenever the Bishop was asked to speak at a dinner, loving his food very much, he would look at the menu to see whether it was worthy of his cloth. If the Bishop thought this not to be the case then he would start his grace: 'Lord, we are not worthy of these, the least of thy mercies.' On the other hand, if he thought it worthy of his position he would start: 'Bountiful Jehovah'.

Tim Brinton, MP

On two occasions I have had meetings interrupted by animals, the non-parliamentary kind. The first time was during a Conservative branch party in Sussex. I was addressing the gathering across a pond in a farmyard when,

60

having just made a rousing Tory point, a lusty cockerel gave loud voice from the barn. The laughter took nearly two minutes to fade.

The second time was whilst opening a fête to raise funds for the Association. I was urging one and all to give generously when I was interrupted by a great deal of barking, as two rival groups of dogs clashed. My comment on both occasions was that people should take no notice, as it was probably only the local Liberal party.

Lord Hooson, QC

During a pro-Boer meeting which was extremely rowdy and restless, a man in the audience threw a cabbage at Lloyd George. He caught it, and, turning it round and looking closely at it, said, 'Ladies and Gentlemen, just as I feared, one of my opponents has lost his head.'

Lord Leverhulme, TD,

A benevolent old gentleman coming home one day, saw, right in front of his house, an overturned load of hay blocking up the road. A small boy was trying to get the hay back into the cart. The gentleman said to the boy, 'Have you to put all that hay back into the cart?'

'Yes, Sir,' said the boy.

'Have you had your dinner?' asked the gentleman.

'No, Sir.'

'Well then, come inside and have your dinner. You will work better for it.'

'I don't think my father would like it,' replied the boy.

'Oh, your father would not mind. Why should he mind

your having a good dinner?'

After dinner he said to the boy, 'Now just you have a walk round my garden and then you will be ready for your work.'

'Please, Sir, I don't think my father would like it.'

'Oh, your father won't mind. He will be glad for you to do it. You have a walk round.' And the boy did. On his returning to the house, the gentleman said, 'Now I have a nice book here. Just look at a few pictures and then you will be ready for your work.'

'But please, Sir, I don't think my father would like it.'

'It's all right, I am sure your father will not mind. But what makes you keep saying you do not think your father would like it?'

'Please, Sir, he's under the hay!'

Dr Immanuel Jakobovits, Chief Rabbi

Three men, having been doomed by their doctors to die within three months, were asked how they would spend the time left to them. The Scotsman answered that he would cheerfully squander his savings on all the pleasures he had previously denied himself. The Frenchman spoke of the utter abandon with which he would dine and wine to his heart's content. And the Jew simply said, 'I would look for another doctor to get a second opinion.'

Richard Body, MP

A former Member of Parliament for the Isle of Wight was not a little taken aback by his reception at the Annual Dinner of one of the Conservative Women's Branches in his constituency – he had begun by saying, 'How good it is to see so many old Cowes faces.'

The Hon. Alan Clark, MP

During the 1922 election Lady Astor was contesting the Sutton Division of Plymouth. She chose, in characteristic and autocratic defiance of the Representation of the People Act, to canvass in the company of the dashing and handsome Admiral of the Fleet, Earl Beatty, DSC, who accompanied her in full dress uniform.

At that time Lady Astor was at the very pinnacle of her physical beauty and she too affected expensive raiment, her grey eyes only thinly concealed by a silk veil, etc. etc. They must have made a most handsome, indeed overpowering, couple.

Lady Astor knocked on the door of a humble house in the Efford district. It opened a few inches. An elderly, but not unworldly face showed itself.

'Good afternoon, I am Lady Astor, your Member of ...'

The door opened and the crone spoke: 'That's right, just along the corridor, under the stairs.'

'No, I don't think you understand. I am Lady Astor, your Member of Parliament, and I am asking for your support in the General Election, which is to be held next Thursday.'

'I don't know nothing about that. My husband just says when the lady comes along with the sailor show 'em to the room under the stairs.'

Reginald Eyre, MP

One day in ancient Rome a Christian was put into the lion pit to await the arrival of the hungry lions. A great beast entered the pit and made his way towards the Christian, licking his lips. The Christian moved quietly to the side of the lion and whispered a few words in his ear. At once the lion turned and slunk away out of the pit. A second lion

63

appeared roaring hungrily but, again, the Christian whispered in his ear and the lion turned and walked disconsolately away. A third lion appeared. Again, the Christian whispered in his ear with the same result.

Nero, who was presiding over the festivities, was fascinated and asked for the Christian to be brought before him. 'Christian, if you will tell me what words you whispered into the ears of those lions, I will give you your freedom.'

'Caesar,' said the Christian, 'it was quite simple. I merely told him that after dinner he would, of course, be expected to make a speech.'

Lord McFadzean, KT

There is the story of the slightly intoxicated policeman who stopped a car and demanded to know if it was licensed. 'Of course it is,' said the irate driver.

'Thank God for that,' said the policeman, 'I'll have a gin and tonic.'

John Page, MP, Chairman, Inter-Parliamentary Union

This story was told by the Leader of a Chinese Parliamentary Delegation, Mr Hao Deqing, at a Parliamentary luncheon given in his honour by the Inter-Parliamentary Union.

This is an old story of a Chinese gentleman who was visiting, for a meal, a friend who was renowned for his meanness. When he was leaving his host took him to the front door, where the guest said, 'Where is the threshold board on your front door?'

The host replied, 'I have never had one here'; to which

the guest said, 'Oh, how silly of me. I must have had too much to drink ... before I arrived!'

Eldon Griffiths, MP

When your Chairman asked me to volunteer to speak tonight he advised me to say just a few words, but like most members of the House of Commons I have never quite known what a few words really means! I was, however, given a definition of this phrase the other night while dining with a Federal Judge in the great American state of Georgia where, as we finished our meal, there was a knocking on the door and there was admitted a most attractive young man with what is known in these parts as a 'Georgia peach'. The young couple asked if the Judge would marry them, to which he replied that unfortunately they would have to wait a few days. Listening unhappily to this, the young man replied, 'But, Sir, could you not say a few words, just to see us through the weekend!'

Sir Angus Maude, PC, TD, MP

A Member of Parliament fell ill and went to hospital. For ten days, he received no letters, no visits, not even a grape. On the tenth day he received a letter on his Association writing paper from his agent which read as follows:

Dear George,
At last night's meeting of the Divisional Council I was instructed to inform you that a Resolution was passed expressing the deepest sympathy with you in your illness and wishing you a speedy recovery. This motion was carried by 28 votes to 19, with 10 abstentions.

Sir Bernard Braine, DL, MP

A fellow parliamentarian, not exactly the most popular of men, was reading *The Times* at breakfast one morning when his eye alighted on the obituary column. There, to his astonishment, was his own obituary. There was no mistake about it – the newspaper thought that he was dead and, what made matters worse, did not seem to think much of him and his life's work.

He went to the telephone and rang a friend – he still had one left – and asked him if he had *The Times*. 'Yes,' replied his friend, recognising his voice, 'I'm reading it now'; and then, after one of those awkward pauses one sometimes experiences in an embarrassing conversation, he enquired, 'By the way, where are you telephoning from?'

Odette (Mrs Geoffrey Hallowes, GC, MBE, Légion d'Honneur)

When my husband attended his school Old Boys' Dinner, I always wondered what he and his friends talked about and did. I was therefore delighted, and honoured, when some years ago a friend asked me to be Guest of Honour at his Old Boys' Dinner.

I sat on the right of the Headmaster, and when he asked me if I was prepared to say a few words at the end of dinner, I moved my head too quickly and my contact lens fell in my soup.

I cannot see with my other eye and am therefore quite blind without the lens, and although I had prepared a short speech, I knew that, even if I could find my contact lens, I would be unable to put it back in my eye. Somehow I managed to retrieve it, slip it into my napkin and then

66

quickly into my bag. To this day I cannot remember what I said, but everyone seemed to be satisfied and happy, even if it was an all-male occasion with a female Guest of Honour for the first time.

After dinner I met many of the Old Boys; to the consternation of my hosts and my husband, when the youngest Old Boy, aged about eighteen, was introduced to me, he asked how old I was. When I told him, he recovered quickly, having seen the shock in the eyes of the other Old Boys, and partially redeemed himself in their eyes when he said, 'If I could take you out for the evening, I would be very proud.'

It showed he had been to the right school, but my husband never quite got over it!

John Heddle, MP

Travelling back from the hustings in Manchester during a General Election campaign, earlier this century, the great F.E. Smith (later Lord Birkenhead) found himself sharing a railway carriage with the legendary Keir Hardie.

Keir Hardie (obviously after a heavy night!) thought that he should strike up a conversation with F.E. and said, 'Cor blimey, Sir, I've got an 'ell of an 'ead', to which F.E. replied, 'My dear fellow – what you need is an aspirate!'

Sir Derek Walker-Smith, QC, MP

In proposing the election of Mr Speaker Thomas in the House of Commons, I told this story of the conversation between a former Ministerial colleague of his and a doctor:

Minister: 'There are two sorts of doctor – the young and

experimental, who kill you off, and the old and traditional, who leave you to die.'

Doctor: 'Yes, Minister, and there are two sorts of politician – those who are dead, and those who ought to be.'

Neil Macfarlane, MP

An eleven-year-old boy was sitting an end of school year examination. The question was asked: 'What is electricity?' After much thought and frequent gazing through the open window, he wrote, 'I did know, but I've forgotten.' When the paper arrived on the desk of the examination marker he penned in the margin, 'Only two people know about electricity – God who can't tell us ... and Tompkins, who has forgotten.'

John Langford Holt, MP

The Chaplain was giving an address to a detachment of soldiers who were about to be dispatched to the front. He ended his address with these immortal words: '... and now God go with you – I will go with you as far as the station.'

Cyril D. Townsend, MP

An elderly Peer was forced to attend a major debate in the House of Lords facing downwards. A colleague commiserated with him but the elderly Peer replied, 'I can assure you, Sir, I have heard some of the nicest things ever said to me in this position.'

Sir Philip Goodhart, MP

In the latter part of 1956, I was visiting Somalia as correspondent of the *Sunday Times*. Our Consul-General in Mogadishu, who was reputed to be the greatest living expert on the Somali language and was the author of the first Somali dictionary, arranged for me to go and see the new Prime Minister.

I arrived rather early at the Government Building, and was for once swiftly escorted through the various layers of attendants. The door of the Prime Minister's office was thrown open. I was ushered in, and found myself in the middle of the second meeting of the new Somali Cabinet.

I sat down in a chair at the end of the table, and the Cabinet looked at me expectantly. It was plain that I was expected to say something, and so, slowly and loudly, I asked, 'What is your economic policy?'

This provoked an animated discussion lasting for almost three-quarters of an hour. It was perhaps the first time they had discussed their economic policy. At last a man who I presume was their Chancellor of the Exchequer turned to me with a beaming smile and said, 'It is to discover oil!'

After I left Somalia I wrote a rather superior and cynical article about basing one's national economic policy on the discovery of oil. I had not then imagined that within twenty-five years it would become my own country's policy as well.

Hamish Gray, PC, MP

The oil industry attracted a number of Southern Scots into my Highland constituency of Ross and Cromarty. One such family enjoying a Sunday stroll in the country was

70

bombarded with questions from their 11-year-old son.

'Hey, Father, what is that four-legged beast called?'

'I'm not sure, laddie,' was the reply.

'Hey, Father, what is the name of that big hill?'

'I am not sure, laddie,' his father repeated.

'Hey, Father, what is the name of that river?'

'I cannot be sure, laddie,' came the answer.

'Now look, Father, you dinna mind me asking all these questions, do ye?'

'Of course not, laddie, if ye dinna ask, you will never learn.'

Sir Geoffrey Howe, PC, QC, Kt, MP

A British businessman had been invited to address a gathering of Japanese tycoons. He knew something of their customs, and particularly that they were a very courteous people. So, on rising to his feet, he bowed deeply to the assembled company. This gesture was greeted with an immense and enthusiastic cheer.

The businessman was so pleased by the response that he bowed to his audience a second time. This time the response was one of sullen, stony hostile silence.

The British businessman turned to his Japanese chairman and said, 'What have I done wrong?'

'These chaps don't like long speeches,' replied his host.

Delwyn Williams, MP

I was in a taxi going round Trafalgar Square when, in front of the taxi driver and myself, a TR7 sports car tried to cut in on a rather large bus. 'Cor blimey, Guv'nor, look at that,'

72

said the irate taxi driver. 'They shouldn't be allowed on our roads.' Inevitably a collision occurred which added to the taxi driver's wrath. 'Now they are holding us up,' he exclaimed. As we got level, it appeared that the two drivers were both coloured gentleman and were engaged in a slanging match. My taxi driver wound down the window and shouted out, 'Driver. Bloody driver,' and eventually one of the coloured men looked up. 'Why don't you both go back then?' he shouted. Thinking he was an irate member of the National Front I sought to placate him by saying, 'Yes, why not send them all back then.' To my chagrin he turned round and said, 'No, what I meant, Sir, was why don't they both reverse their vehicles, that way they will cause less damage.' At which, thank heavens, we both had a good laugh and carried on.

Roger Moate, MP

In thanking you for the splendid dinner tonight, might I say how much better it was than on another occasion when the speaker, having been asked if he had enjoyed his meal, replied:

'If the soup had been as warm as the wine,
And if the wine had been as old as the chicken,
And if the chicken had been as plump and as tender as the waitress,
And if she had been as willing as the elderly dowager sitting next to me,
Then it would have been an excellent meal.'

Ray Whitney, OBE, MP

This is a three-nation story. This time, an Englishman, a Frenchman and a Russian are arguing about what is the most pleasurable experience in life.

The Englishman begins by describing a lovely Sunday summer morning. He rises late, has a leisurely breakfast, just in time to stroll down to the pub for opening time. After several pints with his friends, he returns to a well-cooked lunch of roast lamb and mint sauce with new potatoes and fresh green peas from his garden. He then stretches out for a carefree post-prandial snooze. That, for him, is one of the most pleasurable experiences in life.

'Pouf!' exclaims the Frenchman. 'You English are so unromantic. For me, it is to take a pretty girl, with my wallet full, to my favourite nightclub in Paris, lots of French food, good champagne and soft lights. Then I take her back to my flat for the most pleasurable experience in life.'

'You decadent Westerners do not know that you are born,' says the Russian. 'Let me tell you what real pleasure is. You go to bed at, say, eleven o'clock. At about four in the morning, there is a loud and angry knock at the door of your flat. "Open up, open up," screams someone from outside the door. "Who is it?" you say. "It is the secret police. We have come for Ivan Ivanovich." My friends, easily the most pleasurable experience in life is when you are able to say, "Ivan Ivanovich lives next door." '

Kenneth Warren, MP

A noble Lord espied a hang-glider through the windows of his study and called to his faithful retainer, 'Carruthers, bring me my best pair of Purdeys.' Carruthers duly trundled forward, handed the guns to his Lordship who then went onto the terrace and gave the object in the sky all four barrels. 'Did you get it, My Lord?' the butler asked. 'No,' replied the ageing Peer, 'but I certainly winged it – got it to drop the poor devil it had in its talons.'

Giles Shaw, MP

The Archdeacon had attended the Rotary Club Annual Dinner and was departing relatively late at night in a somewhat merry condition. He passed the entry to an imposing block of flats where lists of cards were to be seen alongside bell pushes. The top name caught his attention. It read, 'St Paul'. With a reverential twinkle, he pressed the bell, despite the lateness of the hour. After a long delay an elderly gentleman, wrapped in a purple dressing-gown, opened the door.

'Is your name Paul?' asked our reverend friend.

'Yes. What on earth do you want at this time of night?' was the reply.

'I just wanted to congratulate you on your letter to the Ephesians,' slurred our respondent.

At which the door was slammed in the caller's face and the Canon tottered off into the night.

Five minutes later he was back, pressing the bell vigorously. The door was opened again, by a more irate version of the gentleman in the purple dressing-gown.

'And what do you want now?' he said.

'Sorry to trouble you,' said our friend, 'but I just wanted to know – did you ever get a reply?'

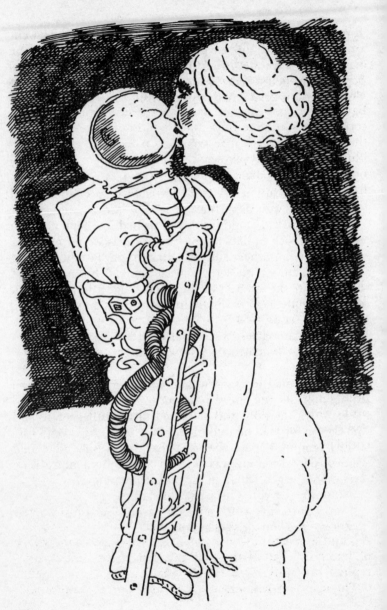

Cyril D. Townsend, MP

A few years ago Jim Prior was trying to reassure an audience which had expressed its concern about the unemployment figures. He pointed out that the Government had taken certain measures and there was bound to be a delay before the results were felt. He went on to use an agricultural illustration: 'If you put a bull in amongst the cows you do not expect immediate results.' At this a red-faced farmer from the back of the hall was heard to comment, 'No, Sir, but at least the cows look happy.'

Sir Peter Emery, MP

The first man to reach the planet Venus stepped out of his spacecraft to be welcomed by the most beautiful woman he'd ever seen: she had a marvellous figure, long blonde hair and aquiline features. He was amazed; not at her great beauty, nor that when she said, 'Welcome, man from the earth,' that she spoke in English, but, that with all this perfect beauty, she stood thirteen feet tall, her delightful proportions towering over him. Therefore when she turned and asked, 'Shall I take you to my leader?' his only response could be, 'Take me to a ladder, I'll see your leader later.'

John Spence, MP

A school inspector asked a class, 'Who blew down the Walls of Jericho?' One of the pupils, a lad called Billy Green, replied, promptly, 'Please, Sir, it wasn't me.'

The inspector was amazed at this show of ignorance and

brought the matter up in the headmaster's study at the end of his visit. 'Do you know,' he said, 'I asked the class who blew down the walls of Jericho and young Billy Green said that it wasn't him.'

The headmaster said, 'Billy Green, eh? Well, I must say that I've always found the lad to be honest and trustworthy, and if he says that it wasn't him, then it wasn't him!'

The inspector left the school without further comment, but lost no time in reporting the full sequence of events to the Ministry of Education in a written report. In due course, he received the following reply:

Dear Sir,
Reference the Walls of Jericho, this is a matter for the Ministry of Works and your letter has been sent to them for their attention.

Neil Thorne, OBE, TD, MP

During the course of the last General Election a young Conservative canvasser arrived at the gate of a recently purchased council house to find the gate closed securely with wire. Undaunted, he squeezed between the privet hedge and the gate post, walked up the path and rang the bell. On looking back towards the gate he noticed, to his horror, his footprints in the newly laid concrete path. Hearing a noise approaching the door he realised that it was too late to retreat and, upon the door being opened by the elector, thought it wisest to announce that he was calling on behalf of the Liberal candidate to seek support in the forthcoming General Election, before carrying out a hasty, strategic withdrawal.

Baron Snoy et d'Oppuers, KBE

The building of Europe came to a deadlock after the vote of the French Assembly on 30 August 1954, which rejected the Paris Treaty on the European Defence Community. It was difficult to imagine then how it would be possible to get it started again.

However, early in 1955, the Benelux countries envisaged a new move, which was called the 'Relance Européenne'. Together, they produced a cautious draft presenting a range of suggestions. The matter had to be submitted to the Council of Ministers of the Coal and Steel Community. But a meeting was difficult to convene – the diaries of the Ministers of Foreign Affairs were too full!

After a great number of consultations, one date only was found to be convenient – 1 June 1955 – but the Italian Minister, Martino, could not at that time leave Sicily, where he was waging an electoral campaign for the Assembly of the region. So, the condition of any ministerial meeting was that it should be held in Sicily. Happily, the other Ministers agreed.

There had been no international encounter in Sicily since the days of Frederic II Hohenstaufen, and nobody knew where the necessary facilities could be found. The only spot where accommodation could be sufficient was Taormina, but the Ministers objected that a conference at Taormina would never be taken seriously. Thus, we took the map of Sicily and found a little town not too near, not too far from Taormina, where it was possible to organise a meeting in the town hall and where we had a relatively easy road to Taormina – this was Messina.

The six national delegations arrived at the Hotel San Domenico in Taormina in a pleasant mood – the Whitsun holiday was just over and many a delegate had enjoyed relaxing in the beautiful resorts of southern Italy and Sicily.

The Belgian delegation, headed by P.-H. Spaak, arrived just at the same minute as the French, which was led by President Pinay, and I remember greeting the French Minister and Ambassador Wormser, together with a gentleman whom I had never met and who happened to be the senior alderman of the city of Saint-Chamond.

The formal meeting in Messina was to be held the next day at 4 p.m. The Sicilian temperature being what it is in early summer, good work could only be done late in the afternoon. We could thus enjoy a pleasant morning without too many duties. At 3 o'clock, the official cars escorted by carabinieri raised a cloud of dust on the road to Messina, and there we listened respectfully to speeches delivered by our superiors. On the second day of meetings, the Chairman, Luxembourg Minister Bech, who was anxious to finish early, turned to me at 6 p.m. and said, 'You have heard the speeches delivered by the members of the Council, now, it is necessary to draft the conclusions of the meetings and would you kindly summon the Ambassadors to a drafting committee. The Ministers will go back to Taormina where you will submit your draft to us, later in the evening.'

Being an obedient Civil Servant, I complied with these instructions, but after thirty minutes, the drafting committee was led to conclude that there had not been a clear understanding between the Ministers and that the kind words which had been exchanged were not sufficient to reach an agreement. We decided to go back to Taormina and report to the Ministers.

I found them sitting on the stone benches of the Greek theatre where the Rome Ballet was to produce dances in the unforgettable surroundings of a proud past. The stars and the moon were shining and the night was bright. I reported to Chairman Bech and explained that we needed a new ministerial meeting. He made such a gesture of despair that I said, 'Why not immediately? Perhaps after the ballet.' He replied, 'You forget that at midnight we are all invited by the

Italian Government to a dinner party in the San Domenico with all these charming ballerinas.' I answered, 'Well, Mr Chairman, the meeting could be held after the dinner, then.'

And that is what happened. The true Conference of Messina was held at Taormina, on 3 June, between 2 and 4 a.m. and it was serious business, with a lively debate and tremendous conclusions. The result was a communiqué full of substance, which was the starting point of two years of negotiations leading to the signing of the Rome Treaty on 25 March 1957.

I was so happy that I stood on the hotel balcony to enjoy the sunrise on Mount Etna, and called Spaak to share this unforgettable moment. The birds were singing and he joined them with an enthusiastic, 'Il Sole Mio'! Then we heard a window open above us and President Pinay's voice shouting: 'Can't you let people get some sleep?'

And that was how the European adventure began!

Lady Burnett

This is a story told to me by a very old friend, concerning an encounter he had with a local crofter on the Isle of Mull.

The visitor said, watching the crofter painting the outside of his house with a very small paint brush, 'Why do you not use a larger paint brush – it would be quicker.'

The crofter replied after a few minutes, 'Aye, but there is no twice the work to do.'

Lord Porritt, GCMG, GCVO, CBE

At a Veteran's Reunion that took place annually in Chicago, a Chinaman and a Jew used to meet regularly and became good friends. Despite enjoying each other's company, they always seemed to end up quarrelling.

On one occasion the Jew said to the Chinaman at the end of their argument, 'Well, anyway it was your people that were responsible for Pearl Harbor!'

The Chinaman, duly incensed, replied, 'That was the Japanese not the Chinese'; to which the Jew replied, 'Oh, well, Chinese, Vietnamese, Japanese – they're all the same to me!'

A year later the same sort of thing occurred and the Chinaman finished the argument by saying, 'Well it was your people that were reponsible for the *Titanic* disaster, wasn't it'; to which the Jew replied furiously, 'The Jews had nothing to do with it!'

The Chinaman replied, 'Well, Sternberg, Rosenberg, Iceberg – they're all much the same aren't they?'

Sir Anthony Kershaw, MC, MP

At a public meeting, a man was called upon to speak in place of Winston Churchill. He started by modestly saying that he could not understand why the choice should have fallen on him, except, perhaps, that it was because he had been a member of the Tory Party for even longer than Winston Churchill, though not, of course, so often.

Anthony Grant, MP

Whips are totally misrepresented in the eyes of the public. Far from being harsh, flinty men, who bully nervous MPs into Lobbies against their deeply held consciences, Whips are men of supreme tact, diplomacy, and persuasion. This is

82

well illustrated by the following example.

One night, or rather early morning, a Whip had to assemble all his MPs for a vital division in the House. He telephoned one who was in bed asleep with his wife. The wife answered the telephone. 'It is the Whip's office here. There is an urgent vote in the House – will you please ask your husband to come back and vote.' Without putting the telephone down she said, nudging her recumbent husband. 'It's the Whips. They want you to go back to the House.' In a sleepy but loud voice the MP said, 'Tell 'em I'm not here!' 'He's not here,' repeated the wife. 'Well, Madam,' the Whip said in a deadpan tone, 'will you please tell the gentleman who is in bed with you to come back and vote!'

Lord James Douglas-Hamilton, MA, LLB, MP

At the Coronation, the man in charge of the celebrations in London wrote to the Commissioner of the Royal Canadian Mounted Police, drawing his attention to the fact that the Mounted Police contingent would be riding through streets in London, lined by troops, many of whom would be wearing Bearskins, and that horses have a great aversion to Bearskins. The writer suggested that the Mounted Police horses therefore be familiarised with Bearskins before they came.

He got a letter back from the Commissioner of the Royal Canadian Mounted Police, thanking him for his courtesy and thoughtfulness, and saying that there was no problem, because the horses of the Mounties were used to bearskins, with the bears inside them!

Cyril D. Townsend, MP

When a former Pope asked the jazz trumpeter, Louis Armstrong, if he had produced any children, Armstrong replied that, no, he hadn't yet, but that he and Mrs Armstrong were having a lot of fun trying.

Vivian Bendall, MP

A young lady came to see a Member of Parliament at one of his surgeries (a Councillor also being present) and in common with other constituents started her long tale of woe. It should be mentioned at this stage that this story is in no way intended to mock this young lady, nor, indeed, to jest about any problem brought to the attention of the MP by a constituent. The MP thinks, however, that the young lady in question would join with him in finding some humour in her sad case.

She had, sadly, been slightly disfigured on the 'upper part of her anatomy' following cosmetic surgery, and she wanted to consult him as to whether she could take any legal action in order to be recompensed. During the interview the young lady produced, from a brown paper bag, an array of photographs which depicted her plight in full. One question did spring to the MP's mind during the interview – who took the photos? – but in the circumstances he refrained from enquiring. However, his curiosity was soon satisfied as the answer was offered quite casually: 'Of course, I had the photos taken at one of those little booths, at a station, where you can get passport photos taken.' The mind boggles at the thought of a cold, windy winter's day and a young lady braving the elements displaying all to the world with the little flimsy curtain flapping in the breeze!

Ian Stewart, MP

A sign seen above a chemist shop:
'We Dispense with Efficiency'.

Nicholas Baker, MP

A British businessman was travelling with a South American airline on an aeroplane which had two pilots.

The first pilot decided to take a stroll into the cabin to talk to the passengers, leaving his co-pilot in charge of the aeroplane. The co-pilot was suddenly caught short and, leaving the aeroplane controls fixed on automatic pilot, he went into the passengers' part of the plane to the lavatory.

Just at that moment the anti-hijack device, which causes the door between the pilot's cabin and the passengers' compartment to shut automatically and stay locked, came into operation and the door clanked shut.

The British businessman and the rest of the passengers then had the unusual experience of seeing two pilots using axes to break down the door to get back to the controls of the plane.

Ivor Stanbrook, MP

A man, after he got on a train, discovered that it was a non-stop to Sevenoaks and would not be stopping at Orpington. He managed to persuade the train staff to arrange with the driver, unofficially, to slow down, as the train passed through Orpington Station, to a speed at which he could safely jump off. When the time came he opened the carriage door, stepped out and ran with the train a few yards only to be grabbed by a passenger holding a door open in a following coach. He was pulled in. 'My goodness,' said the passenger, 'didn't you know this train doesn't stop at Orpington? It was lucky I saw you running for it!'

Hugh Dykes, MP

A senior politician was on an official visit to one of the newly independent African republics and on landing at a remote rural airstrip, he was invited by the Chiefs to address the assembled natives. He went through the usual ritual phrases – 'marvellous to be here' – 'wonderful country' – 'challenge of independence' – and was happy to note that, at the end of each sentence and paragraph of his oration, the enthusiastic natives shouted out, 'Umbula, Umbula!'

He concluded his speech to yet more outbursts of 'Umbula, Umbula,' and was then driven away to inspect a new farm.

As he was going through the cattle pens with the farm manager, he was very dismayed when the manager said to him, 'Be careful where you step, there is a lot of *umbula* about from the cows.'

Peter Hordern, MP

An Australian came to Britain to see his family, and caught a train from Victoria to Chichester in order to visit an elderly aunt who lived there. He bought a first-class ticket and

boarded the train. However, it was the middle of the summer and the train was absolutely packed. He walked along the corridor and eventually saw a first-class carriage with an old lady sitting in the corner and a Pekingese dog on the next seat. So the Australian entered the carriage and asked her very politely if she would mind if her Pekingese sat on her lap while he sat on the seat. She said, 'Certainly not. My dog is going to sit on this seat and you will have to go and find somewhere else.' The Australian walked across the carriage, opened the top window, picked up the Pekingese and threw it out. There was a startled hush and a gentleman sitting in the opposite corner looked over the top of his glasses and his copy of *The Times* and said, 'You know, you Aussies are all the same, you come over here, you murder our language and then you go and throw the wrong bitch out of the window.'

Robin Squire, MP

A well-known vet was telephoned after midnight by an elderly lady who lived nearby. She complained that, at the bottom of her garden, a dog and a bitch were mating noisily. The vet listened to the complaint and then said, 'Madam, do you know what time it is?' to which the lady replied, 'Well, yes, it's half past midnight.' 'Well why don't you tell them that one of them is wanted on the telephone?' said the vet. 'Will that stop them?' asked the lady. 'Well, it stopped me,' he replied.

Victor Goodhew, MP

The 18th century essayist, Joseph Addison, having been

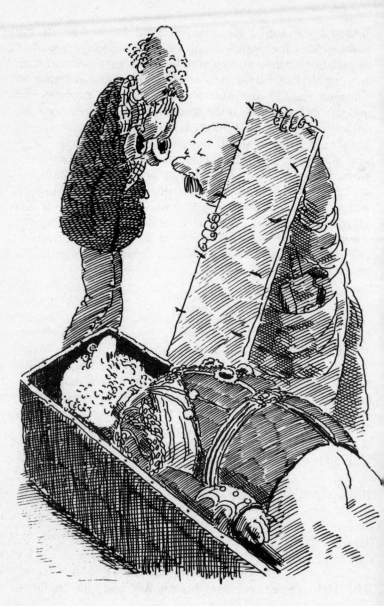

elected to Parliament, rose one day to make his Maiden Speech. Like most other Members in a similar position he was extremely nervous and began by saying, 'Mr Speaker, Sir, I conceive ...' He paused and started again, saying, 'I conceive, Mr Speaker, Sir ...' A sympathetic Member murmured, 'Hear, Hear.' Taking a deep breath, he started once more and said, 'Mr Speaker, Sir, I conceive ...' and, unable to find another word, he sat down, completely lost.

The next Member called by Mr Speaker started, 'Mr Speaker, Sir, the Hon. Member who has just resumed his seat has conceived three times and brought forth nothing.'

Peter Bottomley, MP

During my by-election in 1975, my elderly grandmother came down to help me. I thought that she would be able to persuade people of her own age to consider voting for me, so I rang up the matron of a local old people's home to ask if I could bring my grandmother round. The reply was, 'Even if you get elected and become a Very Important Person, we would not be able to take your grandmother for at least three years, because there is a long waiting list.'

William Benyon, DL, MP

There was once a man whose wife died in India. On receiving the sad news, he asked for her to be embalmed and returned to England. When he opened the coffin he was surpised to find, instead of his wife, a general in full dress uniform.

In response to a frantic telegram, he received the following reply: 'Wife buried with full military honours, you may keep the general.'

John Butcher, MP
A definition of tact: The ability to see others as they see themselves.

Peter Temple-Morris, MP
A complicated legal action, after much argument, eventually found its way up to the Court of Appeal. For the third and final day of the hearing, the client had to leave on important business and requested that the result be sent to him by telegram. He won the case and it was decided that a suitable telegram should contain the immortal phrase, and that phrase only: 'Justice has been done.' The telegram was sent and within the hour an express telegram came back from the client reading: 'Give Notice of Appeal immediately.'

Elaine Kellett-Bowman, MP, MEP
My husband and I both serve in the European Parliament, and, just before Christmas last year, we were attending a function in London to welcome the new French Minister and his wife.

The wife, like all good diplomats' wives, was doing her best to use the language of the host country. She looked at my husband in his pin-stripe suit, turned to me with a beaming smile, and said, 'In London I notice that all well-bred Englishmen come stripped to parties.'

David Mudd, MP

The 1964 General Election was over. The votes had been cast and counted. Labour was in. The Tories were out. The verdict of the Press: 'The Tories lost because they had become out of touch with the people.'

The headlines jarred on the former Tory MP across the breakfast table. 'Out of touch,' he muttered, 'out of touch. How can they say that I was out of touch? Damn it, man, don't these newspaper wallahs know that every Tuesday for the last twenty years I've made a point of keeping in touch by talking things over with all the chaps I've met in the grill room at the Carlton?'

Richard Needham, MP

I had rabbit on Monday,
Boiled rabbit on Tuesday,
Fried rabbit on Wednesday,
Roast rabbit on Thursday,
By Friday I had a stomach ache.
My old girl said to me, 'What you need is Castor Oil.'
I said, 'I don't, I need a ferret!'

Sir Paul Bryan, DSO, MC, MP

Conjurer, to Yorkshire yokel: 'Now, Sir, would you be

surprised if I took a rabbit out of your pocket?'
Yokel: 'I would that.'
Conjurer: 'Why would you be surprised?'
Yokel: ''Cos I've got a ruddy ferret in it.'

Sir John Hedley Greenborough, KBE

A young British diplomat, who was a bachelor, had been recently assigned to a post in a South American country. He was not a particularly sympathetic character and found it difficult to make friends amongst the other members of the Embassy staff, or indeed amongst the British community itself.

One evening the Ambassador was giving a formal ball for other members of diplomatic missions and various other dignitaries. The young bachelor was invited but found himself very much alone and therefore made an early friend of a whisky bottle.

He had partaken of quite a lot when, during one of the dances, he espied at the far end of the ballroom a beautiful svelte creature dressed in a long purple gown. He traced a somewhat unsteady path to this person and said politely, 'Will you do me the honour of dancing this Viennese waltz?'

The reply came immediately. 'There are three reasons why I will not dance with you. The first is that you have obviously had too much to drink. The second is the orchestra is not playing a Viennese waltz – it is playing the Peruvian National Anthem. And, thirdly, I am the Cardinal Archbishop of Buenos Aires.'

Keith Best, MP

A speaker at a dinner droned on at interminable length until one of the guests, seated at the end of the table, could take it no longer. He picked up an empty wine bottle, most of the contents of which he had consumed himself, and hurled it towards the speaker. Unfortunately, being somewhat inebriated, his aim was bad and rather than hitting the speaker the bottle struck the Chairman who was seated beside him. As he clutched his head and sank beneath the table the Chairman was heard to exclaim, 'Hit me again, I can still hear the swine.'

Peter Walker, PC, MBE, MP,

Winston Churchill, when Prime Minister, was approached by BOAC to allow sixty Members of Parliament to go up in a Comet airliner to obtain publicity for the Comet. The Prime Minister replied, 'I think it would be disastrous if suddenly the country were plunged into sixty by-elections, besides which, throughout my long public career I have always maintained that it is unwise to put all your baskets into one egg.'

Mrs Sheila Faith, JP, MP

Joe Bloggs, having been found guilty of theft, was being questioned by the Chairman of the Bench as to his financial situation so that an appropriate fine could be levied upon him.

After asking the usual questions about rent, rates, hire-purchase commitments, etc., the Magistrate asked, 'Do you smoke, my man?'

Joe replied, 'Thank you very much, Your Worship, it's very kind of you, but not just at the moment.'

Iain Sproat, MP

A musician with a tin whistle played right through a village in Aberdeenshire, near where I live, without getting anything for his trouble. As he passed the last door, he turned to a village inhabitant standing there. 'Man,' he said, 'I haven't got a single penny in this whole place!'

'I didn't think you would,' replied the inhabitant. 'You see, we do all our own whistling here.'

Roger Sims, MP

A young woman, possessed of extremely good looks and figure, poisoned her husband, of whom she had tired. Her crime was discovered; she was tried, convicted, and, this being in the days of capital punishment, she was sentenced to death.

On the eve of her execution she was asked if she had any last wish. Yes, she said, she wished to leave this world as she had entered it, unencumbered by clothing. There being nothing in the regulations against this, the Governor consented and next morning she appeared at her cell door and commenced her last walk in, so to speak, her natural state.

As she reached the scaffold the hangman could not help but cast admiring eyes at what he saw. 'My,' he muttered, 'that's a beautiful body you have there.'

'Yes,' came the reply, 'and it's all yours if you keep your trap shut.'

John Cope, MP, Treasurer to H.M. Household

I have changed my job from being an accountant to being a politician, and the difference is highlighted by the story of the tramp on the embankment between Westminster and the City who stopped a man and said, 'Can I have a shilling, Guv'nor? I haven't eaten for a week.' The man was a politician and said, 'Never mind, next week will be better.'

The tramp tried the same line on the next man who came along. This man was an accountant. He adjusted his glasses and asked, 'How does that compare with the same period last year?'

The Hon. Peter Morrison, MP

'Behind every successful man stands an astonished mother-in- law.'

Nicholas Edwards, PC, MP

Winston Churchill was addressing the House of Commons when a Labour Member called Paling shouted, 'You dirty dog!'

'Yes,' snapped Winston, 'and remember what dirty dogs do to palings!'

Kenneth Carlisle, MP

While at University I was asked to speak at my first political meeting. It was held in some remote and draughty village hall a few miles from the University. Apart from the Chairman, only two men, a woman and a dog were present, all seated at the back of the hall. The Chairman rose to open the meeting, and at once berated the audience, fuming, 'If more of you don't turn up we'll never get a good speaker'

David Myles, MP

In the George Orwellian situation of Animal Farm, the hen and the pig were having a discussion. 'I have great difficulty,' said the pig, 'in fully understanding some of these language terms. For instance, what is the difference between participating and being involved?'

'That's easy,' said the hen, 'you know the ham and egg breakfast enjoyed by humans? Well, I participate and you are totally involved.'

Chris Patten, MP

As you may know, Calvin Coolidge was well known for his habitual silence which he justified on one occasion by saying, 'I found out early in life that you don't have to explain something you haven't said.' These silences caused problems at dinner parties. On one occasion, a Washington society leader seated next to the President said, 'Mr President I made a bet today that I could get more than two words out of you this evening.' The President looked at her for a moment and replied, 'You lose.'

On another occasion, seated next to the brilliant and talkative Alice Roosevelt Longworth at a dinner party, even her sparkling failed to thaw him out. Eventually, Mrs Longworth, somewhat exasperated said to Coolidge, 'You must get terribly bored at all the dinners you attend.'

'Well,' replied Coolidge, 'a man must eat.'

John Browne, MP

The Archbishop of Canterbury was due to make an official visit to New York. His advisers were keen to point out the aggressive nature of American radio and press reporters. They briefed and rehearsed him constantly, to prepare him to meet this onslaught.

The Archbishop landed at John F. Kennedy Airport, New York, to be greeted by swarms of reporters. The first question was from a reporter who asked, 'Say, Bishop, what do you think of the large number of brothels on the upper east side of Manhattan?'

The Bishop (thinking rapidly for an evasive and inoffensive answer) replied, 'Are there any brothels on the upper east side of Manhattan?'

Next morning, the headlines of the New York *Times* read, 'Archbishop's first question on entering New York City: 'Are there any brothels on the upper east side of Manhattan?'

Robert Atkins, MP

Outside a village hall during a recent Election Campaign,

was a Labour poster advertising a meeting. It was headlined: 'Labour will cope'. Underneath it was scrawled: 'Next week, "How to Nail Jelly to the Ceiling"!'

Keith Best, MP

An after-dinner speaker went on at great length until, one by one, all the guests had tiptoed out of the room leaving alone the speaker and one solitary guest at the table. The speaker thought it was right that, during the course of his remarks, he should pay tribute to this one individual who had remained to listen. 'I should like to thank you so much for staying to hear me,' said the speaker, to which he received the reply: 'That's quite all right, I am the next speaker!'

Kenneth Baker, MP

When Enoch Powell reached the Pearly Gates he knocked on the door and expected admittance. After a time he heard a voice from the other side saying, 'Who dat down der?' When Enoch heard this he replied, 'Oh, don't bother!'

John Heddle, MP

Lord Justice Ackner, when replying to a toast proposed by the Hon. Member for Lichfield and Tamworth at the Tallow Chandlers Hall in the City of London recently, said, 'I don't know why barristers who earn their living speaking for others should always be in such demand as after-dinner

101

speakers. After all, surgeons, after performing the most intricate operations in the surgery during the day, don't go home and start knitting.'

John Cope, MP, Treasurer to H.M. Household
A farmer won an enormous sum on the football pools. The local newspaper reporter came and asked him what he was going to do with the £½ million and he said, 'I think I'll just carry on farming until it's all gone!'

Dennis Walters, MBE, MP
'All this talk of pre-marital relations! I never went to bed with my wife before we were married. Did you, Bishop?'
  'I don't think so. What was her maiden name?'

John Wakeham, PC, MP
Some years ago a pioneer BBC broadcaster told of sitting next to Winston Churchill while he was giving a splendid oration to a small group. The broadcaster noticed that what appeared to be notes in Churchill's hand was only an ordinary laundry slip, and he commented on this later in private to the great statesman. 'I know,' said Sir Winston, 'but it gave confidence to my audience.'

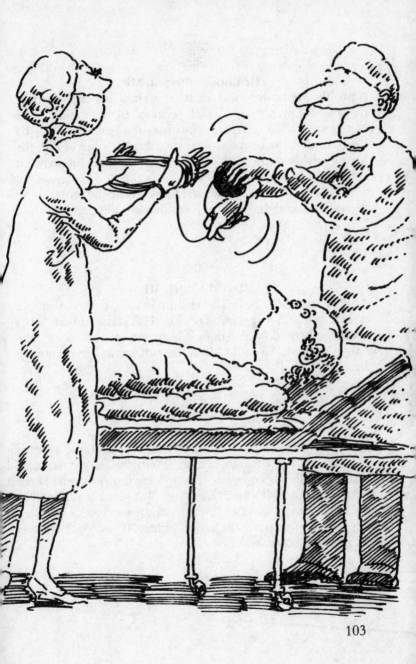

Dr Rhodes Boyson, MP

A prolific Methodist local preacher arrived at a chapel where he was to preach a special sermon by invitation. The Minister of the chapel, knowing the preacher to be long-winded, was anxious to give him a hint about the length of his sermon. 'Now tell me,' he said, 'upon what subject do you intend to speak?'

'Upon the milk of human kindness,' came the reply.

'Indeed,' said the Minister, 'condensed, I hope?'

David Madel, MP

An English fielder near The Hill in Sydney, missed a simple dolly catch and a spectator on The Hill shouted out, 'That was bad, I could have caught it in my mouth!' To which the fielder replied, 'So could I if my mouth was as big as yours.'

John Watson, MP

When passing sentence on a criminal before him, a Leeds Magistrate is quoted as saying, 'Well, this is going to be difficult. I do not know whether you are guilty or not. There is an element of doubt in this case. But you are not getting the benefit of it. I am sending you to prison for six months. If you are guilty you have got off lightly. If you are innocent, let it be a lesson to you.'

James F. Pawsey, MP

Shortly after my election I accepted an invitation to visit one of my First Schools, that is, a school catering for children aged five to eight. I was introduced by the Head Teacher to her five-year-olds as Rugby's new MP, and she asked her children what MP stood for. After some shuffling of feet a little boy put up his hand and said that he thought it stood for 'Military Police'. A little girl then volunteered her view that it stood for 'Missing Persons'. After even more shuffling of feet and hesitation a very timid little boy put his hand up and said that MP stood for 'More Pawseys'!

(James Pawsey is the proud father of 6 sons.)

Sir Dudley Smith, MP

I am a Member of Parliament and I work at the House of Commons. You probably all have your own ideas of what the House of Commons is like. It has been described to me as the only lunatic asylum in the country which is run by the inmates.

Tristan Garel-Jones, MP

A baker in Caernarvon in North Wales was known as 'Dai the Crust'. During the Investiture of the Prince of Wales he baked some special rolls to commemorate that occasion – ever since when he has been known as 'Dai the Upper Crust'!

Sir John Nott, PC, MP

Two of my constituents in Cornwall went on a package tour to Canada. As part of their trip, they were taken to see the Niagara Falls. Unfortunately, their Canadian guide belittled the size and importance of Cornwall beside the huge wealth and natural glories of Canada. On pointing out the Niagara Falls, the Canadian guide said, 'Look at that magnificent sight. You have not got anything like that back in Cornwall, have you?' To which the Cornishman replied, 'No, that's right, but we have got a couple of plumbers who could put it right!'

John Patten, MP

A midwife in a backward and mountainous part of the province, where electricity supplies were fairly rare, was attempting to deliver a baby in a dark and poorly lit room. To help matters, she asked the husband to go and get a lantern from the barn. With the aid of the additional light, she delivered a fine baby. She was clearing up afterwards when suddenly there was a bit more movement and, lo and behold, now there were twins. Shortly afterwards, the same process occurred and there were triplets. As the mother was given the fourth child to appear, she lay back exhausted and shouted at her husband, 'For heaven's sake, take that lantern away, can't you see the light is attracting them!'

Robert Atkins, MP

A strong man in a cabaret act squeezed all the juice out of a lemon and regularly challenged all comers to squeeze any more, for a £50 prize. No one ever did it, until one day an insignificant-looking chap stepped up to the stage, accepted the offer and, without trouble, squeezed at least half a cup more juice. Everyone was amazed, especially the strong man. 'Who the devil are you?' he asked. 'I am Ian ——, Chairman of the Finance Committee of the local Borough Council!'

Humphrey Atkins, PC, MP

A Royal Ulster Constabulary Police Cadet was undergoing an oral test.

INSTRUCTOR: 'You are travelling in your car down a country lane at 40 miles per hour. You pass some hooded men in a ditch who jump out, get into their car and start off after you. What would you do?'

POLICE CADET: 'Eighty!'

Eamon Kennedy, PhD, Ambassador, Irish Embassy

Although former United States President Theodore Roosevelt could shoot fast from the lip with the 'retort proper', an Irishman, who was feeling no pain at the time, once got the better of him in a Boston campaign speech exchange. Republican candidate Theodore Roosevelt was constantly interrupted by the loquacious Irishman, who kept shouting, 'Me, I'm a Democrat'. Finally, Roosevelt asked the Irishman why he was a Democrat. 'My grandfather was a Democrat,' replied the Irishman, 'my father was a Democrat, and I am a Democrat.' Saracastically, Theodore Roosevelt then asked, 'My friend, let's suppose your grandfather had been a jackass, and your father had been a jackass. What would you be?'

Instantly, the Irishman replied, 'Sure, wouldn't that make me a Republican?'

Geoffrey Finsberg, MBE, MP,

An insurance agent was talking to Mr Smith whilst paying his claim in respect of his factory which had been burned down. The insurance agent said to Mr Smith, 'I notice that you increased your fire insurance on the 1st August from £10,000 to £100,000 and that your premises were burnt down on the 3rd August. Why this delay?'

Sir Paul Hawkins, TD, MP

When rabbits were a staple item of commerce in Norfolk, a baker in Thetford had such a reputation for his rabbit pies that he was getting large orders for them from the Norwich shops. One day a close friend of his complained, 'Jack, I can't make out what ha' come oover them rabbit-pies o'yours. They dorn't fare so tasty as to what they used to.'

The baker said confidentially, 'Well, y'see Jimma, tha's all a question o' what tha' Government call supply an' demand. The fac' o' the matter is, I can't git rabbits enow for all o' my customers.'

'So, what are yes a-duin' on?' asked Jimmy.

'Bor,' replied the baker in a whisper, 'atween yew an' me an' the gaatepost, I're had to fill out them pies wi' a mite o' hoss meat.'

'Blast,' said Jimmy. 'How much hoss meat d'yew reckon to put in?'

''Bout fifta-fifta,' whispered the baker, with a grin.

'What d'yew mean by fifta-fifta?' asked Jimmy suspiciously.

'Oh, one hoss, one rabbit,' said the baker.

Lord Shinwell, PC, CH

The prize in the Lincolnshire Young Farmers' raffle was a Mediterranean Cruise. The penalty for the girl who won was to keep a diary. The diary read as follows:

1st Day: Went on board ship.
2nd Day: Asked to sit at the Captain's table.
3rd Day: Went on the bridge.
4th Day: Captain makes improper sugestion.
5th Day: Captain says that if I don't he'll sink the ship.
6th Day: The day I save 866 lives.

Lord Hastings

A Minister was reading a speech blind, from a brief, not having had time to rehearse it with the personal assistant who had written it for him. All went well until he got to the peroration at the end which gave an excellent summary of the great burning question of the day and ended with the rhetorical question, 'And, what, Ladies and Gentlemen, is the answer to these great burning questions?' He turned the page and read, 'You tell 'em – I quit!'

109

David Trippier, JP, MP

On a recent Parliamentary Defence trip I had occasion to be invited into a submarine. Never having been in one before, I turned to a Chief Petty Officer and said, 'For goodness' sake, don't let me touch anything I shouldn't as this is the first time that I have been in one of these.' With a pained expression, reserved for visiting Members of Parliament, the Petty Officer said, 'In your case, sir, count the number of times we dive then add on the number of times we surface, divide by two and if there is one left over don't open that ruddy hatch.'

Lord Charteris of Amisfield, PC, GCB, GCVO, OBE

A small boy on being told by his teacher that one rabbit could reproduce itself a hundred times in a year said, 'My word, I wonder what a married rabbit could do!'

Lord McFadzean, KT

Old Scottish prayer before the Union of Parliaments:
God bless the Houses of Parliament and over-rule their deliberations to the benefit of the common people.

James Prior, PC, MP

Specifications for a 'Harmonised European'. He must have:

The Sense of humour of the German
Humility of the French
Generosity of the Swiss
Taciturnity of the Italian
Political intelligence of the Irish
Diligence of the British
(Not yet approved by the European Parliament!)

Lord Rugby

A door-to-door brush salesman arrived at a remote cottage in the country. The doorbell was answered by an elderly lady who was very reluctant to spend any money and remained impervious to all his most persuasive arguments. Finally, as she turned her back to go into her cottage, he had a sudden inspiration. Would she be interested in a lavatory brush? Although in this primitive setting it seemed highly unlikely, nevertheless he just happened to have one and it was now, as he explained, a very popular selling line. Amazingly, her interest was caught and after a little thought she bought it.

A year passed by and once more he called at the cottage. His first question naturally was about that brush. Had she found it satisfactory? 'Indeed, yes,' she replied, 'I like it very much but my husband, he's so old-fashioned you know, he still prefers toilet paper.'

Lord Charteris of Amisfield, PC, GCB, GCVO, OBE

'His knowledge of religion is limited to his belief that the Epistles were the wives of the Apostles!'

Sydney Chapman, MP

I was asked by the local press for a comment upon a recent Cabinet re-shuffle, I always knew the Prime Minister occupied the seat to the immediate south of mine, and was delighted to see that the new Chairman of the Conservative party occupied that to the north. 'Have you ever felt you're being watched?' asked the reporter. I could only repeat what my wife had said that morning at breakfast: that it was not a case of being watched, but that once again I was being overlooked.

Lord Carrington, PC, KCMG, MC

A certain very bossy and much-disliked Governor's wife at a reception one night sent the ADC to enquire the name of a tune which the band was playing, and to which she had taken a fancy.

The ADC went, and on returning she said to him, 'Captain Smith, what was the tune called?' At that moment there was a dead silence throughout the room, and in ringing and soldierly tones the ADC was heard to say, 'You will remember my kisses, Your Excellency, when I have forgotten your name.'

David Mitchell, MP

The Chairman of the County Council was waiting for a train in a country station. It arrived with two coaches which seemed to be packed, followed by two goods wagons and an empty coach. He entered the latter, and sat down, only to be joined moments later by the superintendent of a local mental asylum and fifteen of his charges. The Chairman considered his position and decided to sit tight, hoping to be left undisturbed.

The superintendent started to check the number of his charges, counting slowly; 'One, two, three, four, five, er, who are you?' he asked.

'I am the Chairman of the County Council,' replied our noble civil servant. 'Six, seven, eight ...' continued the superintendent.

Michael Latham, MP

A barrow boy was advertising his wares outside the hall in which the Labour Party were holding their annual conference. 'Buy your lucky Socialist kittens,' he shouted as he held up a small, black toy kitten for the delegates around to see. Some duly paid eighty-five pence for the mascots.

A week later, outside the same hall, the delegates were leaving the Conservative Party Conference. The same barrow boy was there, selling the same toy kittens. 'Buy your lucky Tory kittens,' he urged. Delegates paid £1 each for their mascots.

A police officer had observed all this, 'Look,' he challenged, 'I saw you last week selling exactly the same toys, but they were Socialist kittens then and no different to the Tory ones you are now selling. What on earth is going on?' 'Oh, well, Officer,' replied the barrow boy, 'the difference is that this week the kittens have got their eyes open.'

David Trippier, JP, MP

Visiting a local church on Easter Sunday, I was treated to a 'blood and thunder' sermon delivered by a visiting Welsh Minister. Half way through his sermon he hammered on the edge of the pulpit with his fist and said, '… and I say to you, if you do not repent of your sins you will surely go to Hell where there will be nothing but fornication, gambling, drinking and loose women', and a voice from the back said, 'O death, where is thy sting?' The Minister went on, 'I have in front of me two glasses, one filled with water and the other filled with gin, and in my hand I have a worm. I put the worm into the water and it swims about happily, but when I put it into the gin you can see that it has died. Now what is the simple moral of this?' … and a voice from the back cried again. 'If you've got worms, drink gin.'

Sir David Nicolson, MEP

A mother was having breakfast with her son when he looked up from his porridge and said, 'I'm not going to school today, Mother,' to which she replied, with surprise, 'And why not?'

'I'll give you three good reason for not going. First, I don't like the boys, secondly, they don't like me, and thirdly, it's a lousy school anyway.'

At this the mother looked at him reprovingly and said, 'I'll give you two good reasons why you are going to school.

Firstly, you are forty-seven years of age, and secondly, you are the Headmaster.'

Cyril D. Townsend, MP

An unsmiling Labour Government Minister in the last
Parliament solemnly told the House of Commons that he
wanted 'the Monopolies Commission to have full
surveillance over contraceptive sheaths, chemical fertilisers
and clutch mechanisms'!

Austin Bunch, CBE, Chairman, The Electricity Council

This old boy with false legs finally took himself to
Roehampton because his tin legs didn't fit at all well. The
surgeon said, 'Oh dear, oh dear, we must take them both
away and adjust them because they are doing you no good
at all.' The old boy said, 'Well, I can't wear my spares, they
are worse than these;' so the surgeon agreed to fit him up
with a pair of peg legs for the interim while they repaired his
proper legs, and he toddled off wering his peg legs and
crutches.

This was Monday. By Friday he was very thirsty, having sat
by the fire all week, and decided he would struggle down to
the local; of course when he got there all his mates were very
sorry for him, and by closing time he was fully loaded. They
pointed him in the right direction to go home and he was all
right until he got to the front gate. He knocked the gate
open with one crutch and steadied himself on the path. Got
his two peg legs up, lifted the other crutch, and
unfortunately the first crutch slipped on a wet leaf and
everything flew in every direction.

After a while the old chap sat up, reached forward and
took hold of one peg leg and then the other. A look of
amazement came over his face and he said, 'What a bloody

116

silly place to leave a wheelbarrow.'

Lord Aylestone, PC, CH, CBE

A Member of Parliament thought that he would considerably improve his constituency support by asking as many questions in Parliament as the Standing Orders allowed. At the following General Election one of his election posters proudly proclaimed, 'Your sitting Member of Parliament has asked 269 Questions in the last Parliamentary Session.' Someone had scrawled underneath, 'He must be b——y ignorant.'

Mrs Reginald Eyre (Actress Anne Clements)

Lady Nancy Astor had a devastating skill at dealing with hecklers. Once, at an unruly farmers' meeting a man called out, 'Say, Missus, how many toes are there on a pig's foot?' She retorted. 'Take off your boots, man, and count for yourself.'

Tony Speller, MP

I have found great amusement in various pieces that have appeared in the press, for instance:

WANTED: Man to work on nuclear fissionable isotope molecular reactive counters and three-phase cyclotronic Uranium photo-synthesisers. No experience necessary.

Students who marry during their courses will not be

permitted to remain in college. Further, students who are already married must either live with their husbands or make other arrangements with the dean.

HEADLINE: NOTED GEOLOGIST STONED AT ROCK FESTIVAL

At a meeting to discuss the route of a proposed ring-road, the highways committee chairman said, 'We intend to take the road through the cemetery, provided we can get permission from the bodies concerned.'

NOTICE: BEWARE, TO TOUCH THESE WIRES IS INSTANT DEATH
Anyone found so doing will be prosecuted.

Alexander Pollock, MP
An old lag was in the dock in the Edinburgh Sheriff Court facing a charge of stealing a pair of trousers. To his surprise the Judge found the charge 'not proven' and told the accused that he was discharged. The man, however, seemed reluctant to leave the dock. His lawyer then urged him to go, but still he declined. 'Why ever not?' asked the lawyer. 'Because I'm wearing them now,' came the reply.

Mrs Reginald Eyre (Actress Anne Clements)
Being an actress I am very fond of stories about the theatre, and members of my profession who, even in adversity, retain a ready wit. Recently I overheard two actors talking of the proposals for the new fourth television channel; one actor thought it splendid. 'Yes,' the other agreed, 'I can see a

118

whole new field of unemployment opening up.'

Nicholas Scott, MBE, MP

When called on as the last speaker:

'I feel rather like the No. 11 bat whose prowess was such that, as he walked out to the wicket, the horse walked over to the roller – so sure was he that the proceedings were about to come to a sudden end!'

Robert Atkins, MP

Mr Kruschev was discoursing at great length, and very critically, about the iniquities of Stalin, when a voice from the large meeting yelled, 'As one of his colleagues at the time, why didn't you stop him?'

Imagine, in Russia, under Mr Kruschev, the terrible, unbearable silence. Tension mounted, the atmosphere could be cut with a knife. Then Mr Kruschev thundered, 'Who said that?' Not a man so much as moved, let alone owned up. Then after a long, long silence Mr Kruschev said quietly, 'Now you know why!'

Nicholas Scott, MBE, MP

I feel rather like the eminent Bishop, who, when asked to respond to the Toast to the Guests after a long list of other after-dinner speakers, rose to say that he had been unsure whether a short speech (cheers!) or a lengthy speech (groan) was necessary and so he had prepared both, and would deliver both of them (deathly hush). The short speech was 'Thank you'. The long speech was 'Thank you very much'. He sat down to deafening cheers!

The Viscount Whitelaw, PC, CH, MC, MP
To the Captain of the Royal and Ancient Golf Club: You were elected and paid to look after my interests. This you have consistently failed to do for fifteen years. Now I understand that you are to amuse yourself at my expense playing golf. I hope you lose your balls!

Robert Atkins, MP
Parliament without a Whip's Office is like a city without sewerage.

The Earl Waldegrave, KG, GCVO, TD, DL
All the economists laid end to end would reach ... no conclusion.

Roger Moate, MP
'A politician is someone who approaches every subject with an open mouth.' (*Oscar Wilde*.)

A young pupil arrived at school and said, 'I am sorry I am late, Miss, but my father got burnt this morning.'

'I am very sorry to hear that, Johnny,' she replied, 'I hope it is not serious.'

'Serious? They don't muck about up at the crematorium.'

Jim Spicer, MP

Soon after the War, Marshal Tito was invited to London and obviously given the red carpet treatment. He sailed down the Thames on a special barge with contingents of all the armed services and volunteer forces drawn up on one bank of the river. A contingent of the then Women's Volunteer Services formed part of the general parade.

Remember how strange and formidable the WVS of the wartime looked: thick lisle stockings, long skirts, hats pulled firmly down and very tight jackets. The following conversation ensued:

President Tito (through interpreter): 'And what are these?'

Pause.

'These, Sir, are the Women's Voluntary Services.'

There was a longer pause before Tito replied, 'In that case I think I would rather pay.'